A NEW ROAD FOR AMERICA

THE NEOLIBERAL MOVEMENT

Edited By Charles Peters and Phillip Keisling

Madison Books

LANHAM • NEW YORK • LONDON

Copyright © 1985 by
Madison Books,
a division of University Press of America,™ Inc.

4720 Boston Way
Lanham, MD 20706

3 Henrietta Street
London WC2E 8LU England

All rights reserved
Printed in the United States of America

Co-published by arrangement with
The Washington Monthly

Distributed to the trade by the Scribner Book Companies.

Library of Congress Cataloging in Publication Data
Main entry under title:
A New road for America.
Includes bibliographies.
1. Liberalism—United States—Addresses, essays,
lectures. 2. United States—Politics and government—
1981-   —Addresses, essays, lectures. I. Peters,
Charles, 1926-   II. Keisling, Phillip.
JA84.U5N395   1985   320.5'13'0973   84-26118
ISBN 0-8191-4087-2 (pbk. : alk. paper)

All books published by Madison Books are printed on
acid-free paper which exceeds the minimum standards set by
the National Historical Publications and Records Commission.

Acknowledgments

Any conference that draws 350 participants and more than 50 panelists from around the country requires a great deal of work. Our task was further complicated, for several reasons. This was the first conference ever held on "neoliberalism"; we had no precedents to follow. Secondly, while preparing for this event we also had to maintain our publishing schedule for *The Washington Monthly*. Without the forebearance and extraordinary efforts of our colleagues at the magazine, the conference couldn't have been possible.

There are many individuals who deserve special recognition; at the risk of embarrassing omissions, they deserve mention here. James Rice, our publisher, along with Nancy Folger and Shela Turpin-Forster, gave generously of their time in planning and promoting the conference. Leslie Winick, who came to our aid on short notice, was instrumental in working out its countless logistical details. Carol Trueblood, who has been a pleasure to work with for more than 20 years, was, as usual, tireless and unselfish in helping with all aspects of the conference. We are also particularly grateful to Stuart Bloch, whose generous financial assistance made it possible to transcribe the conference's proceedings.

Thanks are also in order to all the panelists and participants. The former came despite the absence of any honoraria, and often at considerable personal expense. Though space considerations have forced us to edit and condense their remarks, we hope we have done them justice. Our audience members were a large part of the conference's success; their comments and insightful questions, many of which are reproduced here, enriched the sessions immeasurably.

Finally, we'd like to thank all the journalists who helped us. Some, like Walter Isaacson of *Time* and Ken Auletta of *The New Yorker*, do not ascribe to the "neoliberal" label. They graciously agreed to participate because of their interest in this movement and its possibilities. As for the current and former editors of *The Washington Monthly*, they are a remarkable group of people. Their journalistic efforts have made the magazine successful; we daresay that they, more than anyone else, have also made "neoliberalism" a political force of growing importance.

—Charles Peters
Phillip Keisling

Table of Contents

Introduction

Charles Peters

"Neoliberalism" may be an awkward label, but I have no doubt that the movement which it describes will soon become a major force in American politics. However one assesses the "new ideas" of Gary Hart—whom many have called a neoliberal—his surprisingly strong candidacy in 1984 graphically reveals the extent to which the public is dissatisfied with the responses of both traditional Democrats and Republicans. And it's not only new ideas that voters seem anxious for, but a new vision of politics that better addresses the nation's fundamental problems— defense, entitlement spending, health care, education, to name but a few.

Neoliberalism is dedicated to developing such a vision. But like any movement still in its infancy, there is as yet no agreement even on what a neoliberal is, much less any consensus on a comprehensive platform. Rather than an organized party, so far we are nothing more than a collection of journalists, academics, politicians, government officials, and concerned citizens, linked together by a common belief in the growing obsolescence of conventional politics.

Still, a working definition of the movement is in order, and I offered one in "A Neoliberal's Manifesto," which appeared in the May, 1983 issue of *The Washington Monthly:*

"If neoconservatives are liberals who took a critical look at liberalism and decided to become conservatives, we are liberals who took the same look and decided to retain our goals but to abandon some of our prejudices. We still believe in liberty and justice and a fair chance for all, in mercy for the afflicted and help for the down and out. But we no longer automatically favor unions and big government or oppose the military and big business. Indeed, in our search for solutions that work, we have come to distrust all automatic responses, liberal or conservative."

During the weekend of October 21–23, 1983, *The Washington Monthly* sponsored the first conference on neoliberalism. The turnout—more than 350 people—was itself a heartening sign of interest; we had expected less than half that number. Accounts of the conference subsequently appeared in *The New York Times, Newsday, The New York Daily News, Commentary, The Nation, The Washington Times, The Village Voice, Dissent, The Boston Phoenix,* and *The American Spectator.* In addition, neoliberalism and *The Washington Monthly* have been featured in *Esquire, Newsweek,* the *Columbia Journalism Review,* and in a recent book by Randall Rothenberg.

The heart of the conference lay in 8 panel discussions that focused on the areas neoliberals have explored at greatest length: education, law and the courts, health care, values, national security, entitlements, democratic accountability, and economic growth. More than 40 panelists participated, and the difficult task of selecting them from among many qualified speakers was done with an eye toward conveying the various purposes and characteristics of the movement. The large number of journalists reflected the important role that the *Monthly* and other publications have played in exploring these major issues; it also acknowledged the movement's larger emphasis on the pursuit of facts and analysis that break free of ideological blinders. Academic panelists such as James David Barber, Amitai Etzioni—who originally suggested the conference—and Mancur Olson showed the importance we place on theory and scholarly research that shed light on political questions. There were as many relative unknowns on our panels—including the president of a union local and a high school principal from North Carolina—as there were nationally-known politicians. We chose panelists from among the faithful as well as the skeptical, actively seeking some for their differences with neoliberalism, ranging from a self-described "socialist entrepreneur" to several libertarians.

Most important, we looked for panelists with actual experience in the field, whose opinions and insights were informed by a dedication to putting their ideas into practice. During the arduous process of assembling the panels and coping with last minute cancellations and scheduling difficulties, we often joked that one Donald Burr was worth several Congressmen. Burr, one of our panelists on economic growth, is the president of People Express, a highly successful airline that is substantially owned by its employees. Other "practitioners" included Bill Honig, California's Superintendent of Public Instruction, and Peter Shapiro, the county executive of Essex County, New Jersey. Likewise, we were especially disappointed when several others such as Lee Brown and Billy Reagan—Houston's chief of police and superintendent of schools, respectively— were unable to attend.

In holding the conference, we had several purposes in mind. The most obvious one was simply to plant the flag, to identify and attract others who shared our concerns. We also wanted to dispel some of the misconceptions that have arisen about neoliberalism because of reports in the press and the comments of those who are less than enthusiastic about our efforts. For example, some critics have dismissed us as "Atari Democrats" for our supposed faith in high technology as a panacea for our economic ills. Yet not a single one of our panelists endorsed this vision of economic revitalization; in fact, several explicitly rejected it in outlining the importance of reviving our basic industries. Likewise, neoliberalism has been often associated with calls for a federally managed "industrial policy" that critics say will direct public capital to "winners and losers" based on an assessment of an industry's prospects. Some, like Robert Reich of Harvard, do advocate an aggressive federal role, but many others (myself included) believe that the best "industrial policy" is one that focuses on encouraging risk-taking entrepreneurs and investment in new factories and housing — and discouraging the useless asset shuffling epitomized by corporate mergers and real estate speculation.

Finally, we sought to subject the movement to the hard scrutiny of some of its critics. One of neoliberalism's tenets of faith is the importance of challenging widely-held assumptions, so it was only fitting that we apply the same standard to ourselves. To this end, the conference concluded with a critics' panel moderated by Morton Kondracke of *The New Republic*. Victor Navasky, editor of *The Nation*, and Irving Kristol, a leading neoconservative who edits *The Public Interest*, offered thoughtful and pointed critiques of the weekend's proceedings.

Soliciting criticism, of course, has its pitfalls. One is that some critics may base their case on a faulty reading of your movement. I felt this most keenly when Earl Ravenal, a libertarian on the national security panel, berated the movement's military reformers for their alleged failure to address larger issues such as our global commitments. As the editor of a magazine that has published at least a half dozen articles in this area — with such deliberatively provocative titles as "Get the U.S. out of NATO" and "Forget the Persian Gulf" — it was not easy to resist the urge to interject myself into the discussion.

A more understandable criticism involved the existence of a neoliberal foreign policy. We did not have a separate panel on the subject, so many assumed that this is an area in which we have little or no interest. That is not true. Rather, many of us differ little from traditional liberals on such matters as the insanity of the nuclear arms race, the importance of foreign aid to the Third World, and our antipathy to exercising our military power abroad. As for protecting American interests in an often hostile world, we prefer the kind of response that was exemplified by President Kennedy's naval blockade during the Cuban missile crisis. The threat to our interests was real, but this tough minded and effective response involved no spilling of blood. I personally feel that a similar response was appropriate to the most important foreign policy crisis in the last ten years — the OPEC actions of 1973 and 1979 that caused worldwide inflation and brought us closer to a major depression than we have been since the 1930s. Unlike some neoconservatives who suggested military action in the Persian Gulf, our solution was gas rationing of the kind that we had during World War II, which would not have killed anyone but would have caused, I believe, the collapse of OPEC.

Still, some of the critics made telling points. One that recurred several times during the conference related to the absence of women, blacks, and minorities from our panels as well as the audience. This was partly due to bad luck; Betty Friedan was forced to cancel at the last minute, and such blacks as Lee Brown and William Raspberry of *The Washington Post* had unavoidable schedule conflicts. But the low involvement of women and the non-involvement of minorities was something we were not proud of. I believe neoliberalism has broad appeal; in fact, in its opposition to meaningless credentialism and the emphasis it puts on economic growth, I think it offers more hope to the poor than conventional liberalism. The challenge we now face — perhaps the most important one — is how to broaden the movement to include these voices.

If any one theme emerged from the entire weekend, it was the felt urgency of overcoming the politics of selfishness that now seem to dominate American life. What can be done was perhaps best represented by the efforts of one panelist who unfortunately did not have a chance to tell his full story. He was Walter Bish, the president of the Independent Steelworkers Union of Weirton, West Virginia. Bish would not call himself a neoliberal; in fact, he had never heard of the movement until the conference. But his efforts on behalf of his 7,000 fellow employees at Weirton Steel go to the heart of neoliberalism's message. After National Steel announced that it was closing its tin-plate mill in Weirton because profits were too small, Bish and others convinced the workers to accept a 20 percent pay cut and assume the considerable risks of becoming the mill's new owners. The result? The workers still have well-paying jobs, the community which depended on the mill has been rescued, and during the first quarter of 1984 Weirton Steel recorded a profit for the first time in 3 years.

This volume opens with a condensed version of the opening address I gave at the conference and closes with the critics' panel. Between are edited versions of the presentations made during the 8 panels, and, where appropriate, questions from the audience and the responses of panelists. Indeed, among the conference's most gratifying attributes was the keen interest and intelligent questions of audience members. Interspersed throughout the presentations are excerpts from relevant articles that have appeared in the Monthly and elsewhere, plus some background facts that shed additional light on the questions under discussion. As an appendix, I have included "A Neoliberal's Manifesto."

Opening Address

Charles Peters is editor of *The Washington Monthly*

W hen A Neoliberal's Manifesto [*The Washington Monthly,* May 1983] was published, I received a number of warmly congratulatory letters from prominent political figures. But in the months that followed, most of these people seemed less than eager to wear the neoliberal label in public. I was reminded of the person who, in a similar situation, wrote, "I have always been a secret admirer of yours—and hope to remain so."

I understand the politicians' problem. Long before I became a journalist I was one of them. It was as an editor that I came up with the word "neoliberal." The occasion was *The Washington Monthly*'s tenth anniversary party, and I was responding to an article that had described us as neoconservative. I said: "We're not neoconservative, we're neoliberal." To that sophisticated audience, the term had immediate meaning. But as a politician in West Virginia, would I ever have gone up Cabin Creek and proclaimed, "We're not neoconservatives, we're neoliberals"?

Of course I wouldn't have, because there is no reason to expect the average man to understand "neoliberal," and that's why I think we've got to find a better word if we want this movement to grow, as I'm confident it can.

The last thing we should want to do is separate ourselves from others by using words they don't understand, for neoliberalism is first and foremost a movement of community. We believe in a society that shares its burdens and rewards. We reject the Me Decade and the proliferation of special-interest groups that was its political manifestation. We reject liberal leaders who cater to the special-interest groups of the left just as we do conservatives who cater to those of the right. We want a leader who will challenge us to rise above our personal and group interests when they conflict with those of the community.

All this doesn't mean that neoliberals don't disagree. There are real differences among us that mean there is little danger the movement will become monolithic. For example, while most of us favor a military or national service draft as a means of bringing people of all classes together in service to their country, some, like Taylor Branch and Michael Kinsley, vigorously oppose the idea.

Some support an industrial policy that would favor certain industries. While others of us agree that there is a de facto industrial policy now that is bad and should be faced and changed, we do not support concentrating our bets on a high-tech future. We believe in a policy that encourages economic growth in the form of letting a thousand flowers bloom because we are not at all sure which ones will be the biggest winners.

I also reject the Atari Democrat label because it implies that our only concerns are economic, when in fact we are committed to a broad program of social justice and rededication to the ideals of the Declaration of Independence.

Which brings us back to what do Neoliberals agree about?

First of all—and most important of all—we are liberals. There are large areas in which we are in almost complete agreement with other liberals—from protection of the environment to opposition to any form of racial, religious, or sexual discrimination.

Second, we are realists. We criticize liberalism not to destroy it but to renew it by freeing it from its myths, from its old automatic responses in favor of unions and big government and against business and the military.

We are trying to expose the unstated principles that dominated and severely damaged the liberal movement in the 1970's. First among these was Don't Say Anything Bad About The Good Guys. Liberals felt that any criticism of the institutions they favored, such as the public schools, the civil service, and the unions, would only strengthen the hand of those institutions' enemies. A corollary was Don't Say Anything Good About The Bad Guys, meaning the police, the military, businessmen, and religious leaders. Liberals tended to think that the police were all brutal, that the generals were all Curtis LeMays, that businessmen were all Babbitts or robber barons, and that clergymen were all Elmer Gantrys or sexually repressed inquisitors, unless, of course, they happened to be black and activist.

Another principle was Pull Up The Ladder. In both the public and private sector, unions were seeking and getting wage increases that had the effect of reducing or eliminating employment opportunities for people who were trying to get a foot on the first rung of the ladder. If, for example, more and more of the library's budget was used to pay higher and higher salaries for the librarians in the system, there would be little or no money to hire new librarians, or even replace those who left. So the result was not only declining employment but declining service. In the case of the auto and steel industries, the continuing wage increases meant that the industries became uncompetitive and went into decline. For a while all this meant was that workers already on the ladder were doing better than ever. There just weren't any new jobs. Then as orders declined, layoffs followed and younger workers began dropping from the ladder. And finally, as whole plants were closed, many who had been pulling up the ladder found themselves out of work, too.

During this time too many liberals followed the Don't

Say Anything Bad About The Good Guys principle and refused to criticize their friends who were pulling up the ladder. Thus liberalism was becoming a movement of those who had arrived, those who cared more about preserving and expanding their own gains than helping those in need. Among this kind of liberal there is a powerful need to deny what they are doing, which means they become quite angry when it is exposed. When *The Washington Monthly* revealed that Washington's black upper class was pouring money into a fancy YMCA for its own use while neglecting the Y (now closed) that served poor blacks, there were howls of outrage. There is a similar reaction whenever we suggest that a poor black child might have a better chance of escaping the ghetto if we fired his incompetent teacher, whether white or black.

The third principle is The More The Merrier. The assumption here is that the more beneficiaries a program has, the more likely it will survive. Take Social Security. The original purpose was to protect the elderly from need. But to secure the widest possible support, benefits were paid to rich and poor alike. The catch, of course, is that a lot of money is wasted on people who don't need it—and a lot of people who do need it don't get enough.

The fourth principle is Politics Is Bad And Politicians Are Even Worse. Liberalism entered the seventies having just depoliticized the last refuge of patronage—the post office—but no one seemed to notice that democracy was the real casualty. If democracy means we are governed by people we elect and people they appoint, then it is a not insignificant fact that the people we elect can now choose less than one percent of those who serve under them. Absent the lifeblood of patronage, the political parties have withered and been replaced by a politics of special interest.

In my own life there were three experiences where the gap between liberal myth and reality was dramatic.

First, as a beginning lawyer in the late fifties, I was assigned to represent a good many defendants in criminal cases—perhaps 20 in all. I came to the experience with the image of "The Wrong Man" in my mind. Remember the Hitchcock film? The police have arrested an innocent man and you are going to be the bright and brave young David who saves him from the Goliath prosecution.

Well, I never *had* an innocent man. They were *all* guilty. The truth is that the police seldom got the wrong man. In difficult cases they usually didn't catch anyone. The people they did arrest had usually been apprehended as they were passing color television sets out the store window.

Yet the wrong man myth continues to dominate the liberal mind. An entire episode of a recent "60 Minutes" program was devoted to such a case. They do happen, but they're relatively rare.

Another liberal myth about crime is that practically all criminals could be rehabilitated. My experience was that this was true of only about half—and they were almost all young, nonviolent, first offenders or people who had committed hot-blooded violent crimes during family arguments.

But the criminals who were guilty of cold-blooded violence were scary people. Several years ago I read that one I defended back in West Virginia had broken out of jail in Washington. I spent the next few days praying that he had not learned I was living here. These are people who could not be rehabilitated by a hundred of the country's most brilliant psychiatrists working around the clock, and they need to be kept locked up—not as punishment but to protect the rest of us.

My second reality experience was getting to know the federal civil service when I came to Washington in the early sixties. I had just left the West Virginia legislature where, as a typical young liberal, I had drafted, sponsored, and acted as floor manager for the state's first civil service law. Now, in my first experience with the executive branch I found the civil service was not at all what I and other liberals imagined it to be. Founded to protect the brave, it had attracted the cautious, too many people who wanted job security more than anything else, too many people who lacked the drive and imagination of the risk-taker, and worst of all, too many people who were not concerned with the public because they were not accountable to the public. They could not be fired unless their agency's budget was cut, and it was to the avoidance of that unhappy possibility that whatever dedication they could muster was devoted.

My third reality experience was with the way the government agency for which I worked, the Peace Corps, was covered by the press. Since the Peace Corps was a liberal idea, we got automatically favorable coverage from most reporters. And the few who were hostile looked only for scandal. None tried to discover what was really happening with our programs.

I started *The Washington Monthly* because I suspected that what I saw wrong with the coverage of the Peace Corps was wrong with the coverage of public institutions generally. I wanted to uncover what was really wrong with those institutions and try to figure out what should be done about it.

I was fascinated by the fact that a lot of energetic and thoughtful young people were attracted to that task, so attracted that they pursued it at considerable financial sacrifice. To me this was the first suggestion of the beginnings of a movement. Then I thought it was a movement devoted to a new kind of journalism combining diligent and imaginative investigation with thoughtful analysis of possible causes and possible solutions. But when I found

we were tending to agree on the analysis, I knew something larger was afoot.

Reduced to its essence, that analysis was that this nation
had become the victim of a politics of selfishness, selfishness that was both personal and institutional. Everyone
wanted his tax break or his wage increase without regard to
whether it was in the interest of the country as a whole.

What we saw as the answer to this problem was a politics of responsibility, of sharing, *of doing our part.*

In the fifties "responsibility" became a code word in the
establishment to communicate that the person so described
could be counted on to wear a gray flannel suit and never
rock the boat. Now is the time to redeem it from that sorry
usage and restore its true power and nobility.

A politics of responsibility would mean that we would
no longer insist on this tax subsidy or that wage increase
without regard to its impact on the national community,
that where service or sacrifice was necessary in the common interest, we would do our part, whether that meant
enlisting in the military for two years or simply reading to
an old lady or giving up our claim to government benefits
like Social Security when we're well enough off anyway
and there are others who need more.

"We do our part." When I was a boy that was the slogan
of the NRA and it stirred something in the average man
never seen before or since in this country. Literally millions of citizens proudly marched in parades to demonstrate their determination to share the burden. And I can
tell you that on Cabin Creek every little store and every
filling station had a sign in the window saying, "We Do
Our Part."

In institutional terms doing our part means forgoing
what's good for your company or your agency when it's
not good for the country.

In electoral terms it means voting for a candidate not

on the basis of what he has done for you or your special group but on the basis of what he has done for the community as a whole. You can't expect a politician to rise above the special interest unless you let him know you'll support him if he does.

Doing our part doesn't mean we have to be suckers. If my rich Aunt Alice has to give up the Social Security she uses to go to Paris, your deadbeat brother-in-law should give up the unemployment compensation he spends in Miami Beach. In foreign affairs, we should say to Japan "we'll do our part in our mutual defense and we'll do our part on free trade, but you've got to do yours too." At home the worker who has taken a wage cut to help his company compete—and I think this is vitally important in many of our industries—has a right to ask managers and owners to take a cut too, and if the sacrifice works, and the company prospers, he gets his fair share of the profits.

A politics of responsibility is going to require a public that knows and understands what's wrong with the government well enough to vote for candidates who can make things right. This means a lot more of the kind of reality journalism to which *The Washington Monthly* has been dedicated. It means radically improved instruction in history and politics in our schools. And I think it means having a radical increase in the number of people who have worked in government.

The best way to learn the reality of government and the problems it faces is to experience it first-hand. That's why I think it is important to open up roughly half of the government jobs to short-term—two- to five-year—appointments to people from all over the country who could not only learn but bring to Washington and to their state capitals a feeling for grass-roots reality that the average civil servant lost long ago.

At the heart of the politics of responsibility is choosing

work that counts. Too many people are devoting their
lives to making money or to achieving the status of being
professionals, or to simply proving they have good taste by
going to the latest "in" place for their vacation or buying
the right car or having the right books on their shelves
and the right magazines on their coffee tables. There's
nothing wrong with making money or being a professional or having good taste if—and this is crucial—it doesn't
divert you from doing work that counts.

Can such radical change as I have been describing
actually take place?

I believe radical change can happen because I've seen
it happen. By 1941 the cruel depression of the thirties
turned into 40 years of prosperity. The vicious anti-Catholic
feeling that cost John Kennedy several states in 1960 had
almost entirely disappeared, thanks to his presidency and
the papacy of John XXIII, by the time of Kennedy's death
in 1963. And who could have dreamed in 1960 that just a
decade later black and white football players would be
hugging each other on the sidelines when Alabama scored
a touchdown?

If you think community is unobtainable, John Kennedy,
in 1946, when he was only 29 years old and campaigning
for the first time for Congress, described how community
had been attained during World War II:

"Most of the courage shown in the war came from
men's understanding of their interdependence on each
other. Men were saving other men's lives at the risk of
their own simply because they realized that perhaps the
next day their lives would be saved in turn. And so there
was built up during the war a great feeling of comradeship
and fellowship and loyalty.

"Now they miss the feeling of interdependence, that
sense of working together for a common cause. In civilian
life, they feel they have only themselves to depend on.

They miss their wartime friends, and the understanding of their wartime friendships. One veteran told me that when he brought one of his Army friends to his home, his wife said, 'What can you possibly see in O'Brien?' The veteran remembered O'Brien in Italy, walking with him from Sicily to the Po Valley, every bloody mile of the way. He knew what he could see in O'Brien."

The politics of responsibility can be accused of being idealistic. And of course it is just that. Remember what Woodrow Wilson said: "They call me an idealist. That's how I know I'm an American." The way we have behaved as a people in recent years has made that line sound naive, even absurd. Let's make it sound right again.

Education

THE PANELISTS:

Phillip Keisling (moderator)
is an editor of
The Washington Monthly.
Bruce Babbitt is the
Governor of Arizona.
Thomas Eagleton is the senior
Senator from Missouri.
Peggy Holliday is the principal of
Daniel Middle School in
Raleigh, North Carolina.
Bill Honig is the Superintendent
of Public Instruction in
California.

Phillip Keisling (moderator): Education is a perfect issue with which to start a conference on neoliberalism, for two reasons. First, I think the sorry state of the public schools—and we've had as many national commissions make that point as we've had Democratic candidates trying to get the endorsement of the National Education Association—is a classic illustration of some of the failures of what I consider conventional liberalism. Secondly, I think that neoliberalism and some of its major tenets offer some hope for reviving the public schools.

On the issue of public education, something interesting has happened: many of the criticisms that are being made of public schools have somehow become the prop-

19

erty of conservatives and the far right wing. I wrote an article about a year ago called "The Class War We Can't Afford to Lose" in which I made the points that it ought to be easier to fire bad teachers; we ought to judge teachers, try to make some quality distinctions in terms of how we pay and promote people; and we ought to bring teachers into the system according to whether they can teach or not, and not according to whether they possess meaningless credentials. I made these points, and lo and behold, about the only people who rushed to my defense after the National Education Association got done attacking me were many people who were tremendously conservative.

This strikes me as such a paradox, because what could be more liberal than being dedicated to quality in the schools, of ensuring that those kids, for example, who are poor and disadvantaged have the best teachers and the best education so they can overcome the other handicaps they have in life? There are a lot of people in America who are going to have their lives ruined by bad schools unless we do something.

In doing my story, for example, I came across a story of a woman named Ruby Bridges. Some of you may remember her. In 1960, as a six-year-old girl, she was the first black child to go into New Orleans' then-segregated public school system. Recently, she took her own kids out of public school in New Orleans and put them in a parochial school. It didn't have to do with religious reasons so much as she didn't want to have her kids, who had finally overcome some of those barriers of racial prejudice, to then have their lives ruined by an inferior education. It's my belief that if Marx and Engels were alive today they'd be writing the Education Manifesto and not the Communist Manifesto. They'd be talking about how our children are being oppressed and kept down by a bad public school system.

Governor Bruce Babbitt: We're in the midst, in my opinion, of the most profound and exciting revolution in American education of this century. The bastions are crumbling, a thousand flowers are blooming, ferment and reform are in the air, standards are going up, teacher compensation issues are being addressed, the shackles of pedagogy are being broken in the universities and in the schools. Things are really beginning to come alive, at long last.

The first characteristic of this revolution is that it is not a revolution led by the academic establishment. It is a grassroots revolution that is, in large measure, being led by the political process *against* the academic establishment. The implications of that, I think, are far-reaching.

The second atypical feature of this revolution is that it's occurring at the state level rather than the federal level. The experts are not leading it, and it's not being led in Washington.

The third remarkable characteristic is that it is very clearly a bipartisan revolution. There are people like Governor Alexander in Tennessee, a Republican, and many, many others. Democrats were a little slow getting started because they were held in bondage by their own constituency—the academic establishment—and only recently have they shown the courage to stand up to their constituency in the academic world and to say the public interest must be served despite your opposition to reform.

A word about the national response. Any reform movement in this country ought to have some aspect of biplay between state and national; that's what a federal system is all about. The national response to this revolution has been sterile, to put it mildly, among both Democrats and Republicans. At the national level, the Democrats by and large remain in total bondage to the academic establishment. The Democratic response at the national level has consisted of candidates attempting to out-bid each other in proposing more money with no reform. You see presidential candidates saying "I bid," literally, at the NEA convention, saying, "I bid $10 billion for your support." Followed by other candidates who say, "No, I bid $14 billion, it will consist of a $5,000 check for every member in the audience." Republicans are scarcely better at the national level. The Republican response has consisted largely of exhortation and rhetoric with no proposals at all, no creativity about what the federal response ought to be.

The federal system is for once working upside down; the action is happening at the state level. Ultimately there will have to be some federal involvement. But for the time being, I think Justice Brandeis was right some 40 or 50 years ago when he wrote that "ultimately the power of this federal system is that reform can come leaking out against all odds." There are 50 states and a national capital; somebody will ultimately get loose and start running with the ball. So I guess that's an encouraging message.

Senator Thomas Eagleton: I'm the federal government representative on this panel and thus have the risky honor of defending, as it were, the federal involvement in education. I can't defend it in its entirety. But I will not shirk from it in its entirety, either. And part of what I say will be at least a partial rejoinder to Governor Babbitt.

Why did the federal government get involved in public education in the first place? In 1965, the Congress passed the Elementary and Secondary Education Act, for one good reason: the states and the school districts had defaulted on their responsibility to bring education to economically disadvantaged individuals. The record was abundantly clear. This wasn't done in haste, nor was it done in anger. It was really done in sadness that a responsibility had been forfeited by those who had been charged to fulfill it.

There may be a grassroots revolt, as the governor points out, in some states, and I dare say it's true in Arizona. But I don't detect, for instance, in my own state a similar grass-roots revolt. I detect people yelling and screaming for better education, but rejecting practically every school tax levy in about 10 years. White, south St. Louis, mostly grandparents, either childless or Catholic, as I am, by faith, with kids in parochial schools, votes 95 percent "no" on any levy in the City of St. Louis. Black, north St. Louis votes about 95 percent "yes," but the levy goes down nonetheless.

Now what kind of grassroots revolt is that for quality education? The City of St. Louis school system is virtually bankrupt. The same can be said of the Kansas City school district, and, for that matter, some rural school districts.

What about this bartering or bidding process of candidates running around offering checks and $14 billion here and there? Maybe it has taken unseemly overtones. But a beginning salary in rural Missouri for a public school teacher is $8500 a year. $8500 a year. The poverty level in this country for a family of four is $9900 a year. What kind of grassroots revolt is going on in my state of Missouri that says you'll offer someone with a college degree to teach your kids a starting salary of $8500 a year? And you want to attract into that profession the best that's potentially available in this country?

Where can you find a chemistry teacher in this country? I had a chemistry teacher from St. Joseph, Missouri, who was named Teacher of the Year and had lunch in the White House with President Reagan. He came in to see me, making the rounds after he got his lovely award from the president. He's also head of the chemistry department. He's the head of a department of one—himself. There's been a vacancy for three years in the St. Joseph School System, a pretty sizeable city north of Kansas City, for a second chemistry teacher. They've not been able to fill it because chemistry graduates, when they come out of the colleges around Missouri, can go with Emerson Electric or McDonnell Douglas or Bendix or any other number of companies. You are not going to take up a teaching job at these penurious salaries that I've mentioned. What kind of grassroots revolt do we have there?

The reason we had quality education in this country at one time is we had indentured women teaching in the public schools. Up until about 15 years ago, really, a woman had two choices when she got out of college: she could be a nurse or a teacher. She couldn't get into law school, she couldn't get into engineering school, she couldn't get into business school. All the various professions, for practical purposes, were denied her. So she became a teacher, and thus were channeled into one market practically all of the educated women in the country. You could pay them whatever miserly salary you wanted to pay them because that's the job they had to take or lump it. That's how we had quality education in this country.

So I'm not shy about saying that salaries of teachers in my state ought to go up by four or five thousand dollars, across the board. You've got to get base pay up if you're going to attract people by and large into the profession. But you need merit pay, too, simultaneously. I don't think that they're mutually exclusive. I don't think it's one or the other.

Merit pay is much cheaper. You can do a merit pay plan for the whole country for a couple hundred measly million, which is chicken feed even out of a Reagan budget. But it will take a substantial investment of megabucks in the megabillions to do something about the gross inadequacies of base pay of teachers across the country. That's got to be addressed, and I think it's going to have to be addressed at least in part on the federal level, perhaps in some kind of a matching program with the states.

Peggy Holliday: As a principal, I have 70 teaching staff working with 1,172 youngsters each day. I cannot offer them monetary rewards for doing a good job.

We have a thing called a "teacher workday" every once in a while. It's a time when the kids take off and go to the state fair or go to visit grandmother on Thanksgiving, or one of those holidays. The teachers sit there and catch up on the paperwork and take a deep breath and get on the phone and call all the folks to come in and speak to everybody, set up field trips, those types of things. So one of the few things that I can do as an administrator to compensate them is to let them out a few minutes early on that teacher workday. Just simply tell them, you're supposed to be here from 8:00 until 4:00; I'm not going to look for you after 2 o'clock, I'm not going to look for you after noon. That's a small compensation. That's the only thing, pretty much, as a principal that I have that I can compensate them with—a little bit of time.

We've got sorry teachers, and we've got some bad ones—God knows we've got some bad ones. And it takes almost an Act of God Himself to get rid of some of those bad ones and instead of maybe firing them outright, there are ways to make their lives tougher. You demand excellence.

I think one of the best things that the federal government ever did back in the dark ages of the late '50s and early '60s was the National Science Foundation—lo and behold, when they started pouring money into education, they poured it into teacher education and not into gimicky programs like we're seeing a whole lot of today. They took those of us who were coming out of the colleges and put us in institutes for six or seven or eight weeks. They didn't talk about motivating the child, and we didn't talk about how to talk to the black child versus the Indian child versus the Hispanic child versus the white American child. Instead, Peggy learned a whole of a lot about organic chemistry and when I went in that classroom I knew my subject matter and I felt secure.

Today, we do not have the indentured women in the profession, thank God. Yet I was one of them. There is a member of this audience, my daughter, who refused to be an indentured woman and go into the field of education. Today she's sitting there with an engineering degree. She would have made one hell of a teacher. But she won't go that route, largely because of the money and because of the working conditions. And I think that we've lost something in education.

Bill Honig: One of the secrets, I think, of doing something about quality education is breaking the traditional, conventional way of looking at things. Before I was elected, the liberals, or the Democrats, in California would not take on the issues of quality. They would not talk about it. Basically the argument was it's a money issue: unless we pay teachers adequately, unless we put more money into the schools, you can't talk about any other area. At the same time, the Republicans were saying get rid of collective bargaining, seniority, tenure, and these kinds of things. That's all they were willing to talk about, though in California, the Republicans were a little bit different than they are nationally, because nationally a wing of the Republican Party is talking about voucher plans or tuition tax credit plans and how you get out of the public schools, while in California, you at least had a core within the Republican leadership willing to go to bat for public education.

Our strategy was fairly straightforward. Number one, you had to go out to the public and present a philosophy of education to get them on board. You could not go out and say, "Give us more money, schools are underfunded, we're destroying education." You had to say, "We're going to make some changes." So we approached the educational community, which did not support me, by the way, in the election. I was almost unanimously opposed by the teacher groups who put a substantial amount of money into my opponent's campaign, and by the superintendents who did not want massive changes.

I happen to believe in a more traditional approach in education—high standards, requiring students to take a full course of study whether they're going on to college or going on to work. Students need to know how to write and communicate if they're going to hold jobs. And that is somewhat opposed to the philosophy that's been in place where there have been a tremendous amount of electives offered, a tremendous amount of choice given students. We had a three-tiered system in education that's been the conventional way of doing it for about 50 years. Kids that go to college get an academic education. Kids that go to work get what they call a general education, and when you do a transcript analysis of what these kids take, it's very, very weak. And then kids that get vocational education courses get technical skills but, again, don't get academic skills.

If we're going to prepare our students for employment, we have got to do a better job across the board, because 50–60 percent of the jobs are going to require higher levels of education. That point was well understood by our business community in California. The other key element of the coalition were the ethnic groups. Now, again, what was holding us back was the idea that if you talked about standards or expectations or poor curriculum, you're elitist, you're racist, that that was somehow against the minority communities. We were able to go to the black groups in Los Angeles, Oakland, San Francisco, the Hispanic groups that had supported me in the campaign. (About 25 percent of our students are Hispanic, about 10 percent are black, about 6 or 7 percent are Asian, and in about five or six years, it's going to be 50–50 (minority-white) and the Hispanics are going to be one-third of all the students in the system.) We were able to go to those groups, make the pitch for the kind of education I'm talking about, and get them on board for our reforms.

We came in with a whole list of reforms. Statewide graduation requirements, which we did not have in California. We had changes in the discipline measures. We had changes in seniority. We made it easier to fire teachers. We had a master teacher concept which avoided the merit pay controversy by saying, sure, we'll pay $4,000 extra to a teacher but we want you to do a little bit of extra work, either teaching new teachers or teaching existing teachers or working in curriculum development. So we stood up with some integrity as a profession and said this is what we're for. And I think that's the secret to gathering, galvanizing public support. You've got to go out to the public and say this is what we're going to do in education, will you support us, will you back us in this effort, and will you pay the price?

The last point I'll make—we talk about the area of credentials and how to attract new teachers, which I think is a major issue to be faced. We can put the kind of quality education in place, we can get it moving in the right direction. But if we can't attract top flight people into the profession, it's all going to be for nought. Only four percent of college students now are thinking about education as a career. Unless we broaden our recruitment pools, unless we raise beginning salaries—which was in the bill—unless we do something about the quality of training and unless we do something—and this is key—about conditions in the classrooms, then they're going to go someplace else. And they're doing that now in droves.

Question: Superintendent Honig raised what I consider to be an absolutely key point—how do you get the best, brightest, most talented people who are now becoming lawyers, accountants, consultants, what have you, into the profession of teaching? We've talked some about money, about raising basic teaching salaries. We've talked some about quality and performance evaluation, about making the choices, who's a good teacher, who's a bad one, getting the bad ones out and rewarding the good ones.

But there's another aspect—credentialism—and I might get some disagreement on this. Do you think we ought to have some fundamental changes in what's required to become a teacher, let's say, in a public high school? Right now, you've got to go through a lot of education courses in college in order to get that certificate, or they don't even allow you in the door. If you can prove you know history from A to Z, and you love teaching, and you're motivated, you still can't teach now unless you have that piece of paper.

Governor Babbitt: The credentialism issue is important. Education colleges have slipped into pedagogy carried way too far. We really need to reassess how it is you get people into teaching who know the subject matter and who have not been deadened with quite so much pedagogy—in fact, artificial and not very useful requirements.

Senator Eagleton: I think it requires substantial changes. I will illustrate it by one flagrant point. We have an institution in St. Louis—I keep harping back to my home state, but that's the state I know best and St. Louis is my home city and thus the city I know best. It's called Harris-Stowe Teachers College.

Heretofore it used to be run by the City of St. Louis School System. As a teacher training ground, the City of St. Louis School System couldn't carry the financial load and the state took it over. But under state law any graduate of that school is automatically put on the applicant rolls of the St. Louis School System. Now, if there are no vacancies, of course, he or she does not get a position. But they are automatically put on the rolls and when a vacancy does occur, if you've got a credential from Harris-Stowe Teachers College, you sooner or later become a teacher in the City of St. Louis. And that is credentialism at its worst.

Mr. Honig: In the bill that passed in California there was a provision which I think is a radical change. You can become a teacher if you have subject matter competence, pass a subject matter test, and if the local district gives you some help in seeing whether you can teach or not. There's also a master teacher that works with you. That's hooking the master teacher concept with the broadening recruitment pool. Now, the bill was compromised in the legislature and they added to that provision that there has to be a declaration of emergency by the local district that you can't find, for example, math teachers. That sounds funny but Los Angeles, for example, cannot find enough teachers; it's the largest district in the state and they're always 2,000 or 3,000 teachers short.

We've also got to make some basic changes in how you educate all students at the university level. If teachers are going to have a liberal education, if they're going to teach, if we're serious about subject matter, about history and literature and English and having some concept of who we are and what we believe in, and that becomes an integral part of the curriculum, then we're going to have to have people trained that way. Most universities are not organized to do that—not with teachers, not with engineers, not with lawyers, not with anybody. There's got to be attention paid to how you get our core ideas across to college students, and an organizational effort to do that. So it's much broader than just the teacher schools.

Question: What's the reaction of the panelists to a voucher system—one specifically targeted to low-income parents?

Governor Babbitt: The answer is no.

Senator Eagleton: I'm enough of a traditionalist to believe that a voucher system, even if limited to low- and moderate-income, would be the ultimate death knell of the public education system.

Mr. Honig: I'm against a voucher plan. I think what you're seeing is a reaction against schools that are not doing the job. There's a much more direct way of doing something about that, which are the things we've been talking about. If we can get quality education, those statistics will be reversed. The problem with the voucher is it may work, but it may not. And if it doesn't, we've destroyed another generation of students and maybe the public schools in this democracy. So it's a high stake issue. I don't think you take these kinds of reckless acts unless you're pretty assured that something will change. I may change my mind if we cannot turn the schools around, because then you do have to take a radical slice at it. But right now I think we've got the commitment and willingness of school people to turn it around and the public will support us. So let's go with a moderate and direct route to make quality education.

Ms. Holliday: At this point in time a voucher system? No.

"If Marx and Engels were living in today's America, they would be writing 'The Education Manifesto.' Millions of our citizens are being oppressed, not by the evils of the capitalist system, but by a public school system that is bad and getting worse. Meanwhile, where are the sons and daughters of what Marx and Engels would call the ruling class, those who not only hold high government posts but are leading lawyers, doctors, businessmen, accountants, journalists, and teachers? For the most part, their children are nowhere in sight in these urban public schools. They've either migrated to the suburbs or bailed out of the public school system altogether. In cities like Philadelphia the mayor and most civic leaders now send their children to private schools; of those who remain in that city's school district, over a third are on welfare. In the District of Columbia parents cajole, plead, wheedle, and pull strings, not to get their children into Harvard, Yale, or even a prep school, but into private elemntary schools that cost almost $5,000 a year. Then there's the National Education Association official who accused Reagan of trying to 'destroy public education' with his proposal to give $500 tuition tax credits to parents of private school students. He, too, sends his son to private school.

"America's public schools increasingly resemble a sinking luxury liner. First class ticket holders have gotten off safely. Those stuck below deck in third class are starting to tread water."

—from "The Class War We
Can't Afford to Lose," *The
Washington Monthly,* June 1982

"The first obstacle (to better education) is a type of school itself—the nation's 1,300 teachers' colleges, whose existence and survival are predicated on the dubious premise that public school teachers must endure a battery of often mind-numbing 'professional education courses' before they can receive their credentials. The result is credentialed teachers who often can't teach. Indeed, this misguided insistence on professionalism is a major reason why the nation's best college graduates are either teaching in private schools—usually for longer hours at much less money—or choosing other professions altogether.

The other major obstacle to improving public education lies in the teacher's unions—specifically the National Education Association, which has 1.7 million members, and the American Federation of Teachers, with about 500,000 members. That teachers have formed these unions is perfectly understandable; during most of this century they have been shabbily treated, grossly underpaid, and subject to the often petty, arbitrary actions of school administrators. Yet as unions, these organizations are dedicated to protecting *all* their members, particularly the mediocre and downright incompetent. As a result, their allegiance ultimately lies with the bad teacher rather than the students who've been victimized by what amounts to educational malpractice."

—from "The Class War We
Can't Afford to Lose," *The
Washington Monthly*, June 1982

BIBLIOGRAPHY

Articles in The Washington Monthly

Aldrich, Hope, "The Day the PTA Stayed Home," June, 1984
Ohanian, Susan, "The Nightmare of Teacher Certification," April, 1984

Schultz, Danielle L., "Lessons from America's Best-Run Schools," November, 1983

Noah, Timothy, "Highbrow Robbery: The Colleges Call It Tuition, We Call It Plunder," July/August, 1983

Vopat, Jim, "Guilty Secrets of an ETS Grader," November, 1982

Keisling, Phil, "The Class War We Can't Afford to Lose," June, 1982

Cramer, Jerome, "One Step Ahead of the Sheriff," March, 1982

Bovard, James, "How Teachers Teach Selfishness," June, 1981

Nocera, Joseph, "Saving Our Schools From the Teacher's Union," May, 1979

Rodriguez, Eric, "Inside the Educational Testing Service—Or the Plot to Multiple-Choice Us From Cradle to Grave," March, 1974

Shapiro, Walter, "Black and White Together Is Still the Point," June, 1973

Other Articles

Boly, William, "Can This Man Save Our Schools?" *California,* September, 1983

Keisling, Phil, "How to Save the Public Schools," *Reader's Digest,* February, 1983.

Owen, David, "Breakdown at Merit Control: The Last Days of ETS," *Harper's,* May, 1983

Books

Boyer, Ernest (Carnegie Foundation for the Advancement of Teaching), *High School*

Coleman, James, *High School Achievement*

National Commission on Excellence in Education, *A Nation at Risk*

Sewall, Gil, *Necessary Lessons*

Law and the Courts

THE PANELISTS:
Robert M. Kaus (moderator)
is a former politics
editor of *Harper's*.
Philip Stern, chairman of The
Project for Investigative
Reporting on Money in
Politics, is a lawyer and the
author of *Lawyers on Trial.*
Justice Richard Neely, a member and
former Chief Justice of
the West Virginia
Supreme Court of
Appeals, is the author of
*How Courts Govern
America* and *Why Courts
Don't Work.*
Robert Nagel is a law professor at
the University of
Colorado at Boulder.
Michael Kinsley is *The New
Republic's* TRB.

Robert Kaus (moderator): We have two main issues to cover in this panel. The first is the issue of crime and what to do about it. The second issue is the general question of legalism. Are there too many lawyers in our society? We all know that there are almost as many lawyers in this room as there are in all of Japan. I believe that has harmed our productivity. So there's a constellation of issues involving overreliance on the courts and legalism.

Philip Stern: I have set out a series of questions that I think neoliberals might ask about law and the legal profession:

Why is it that we have 40 times the number of lawyers per capita that Japan has and three times the number of lawyers per capita that England has?

Why should probate fees here be 100 times what they are in England? Why should we in America pay three times in legal fees for probate what we pay for funeral expenses? Why should lawyers be involved at all in the 90-plus percent of wills that are uncontested?

Why should we pay $1 billion in fees to real estate lawyers when many countries make selling a home as simple and lawyer-free as selling a car?

Why should we pay one-quarter of our auto insurance premiums to lawyers rather that to auto accident victims?

Why shouldn't lawyers be free to advertise in any way that is not misleading or deceptive, or be free to enter into partnerships with accountants or tax preparers in order to offer one-stop service?

Why should our grievances against lawyers be adjudged by bar associations, panels made up of colleagues of the "accused"?

The basic answer to all of these questions, in addition to the fact that lawyers are a powerful component of our society—being numerous in state legislatures and in the Congress—is that we have tolerated the legal profession as a legal, licensed monopoly in our society, and a monopoly not only tolerated by, but enforced by the state.

The most grievous, current example of this is the case of Rosemary Furman in Florida. A former legal secretary, she had the audacity, after the Florida legislature simplified the divorce laws, to begin typing the forms for $50 in uncontested divorces instead of the usual $250 that lawyers had been charging. This brought upon her the wrath of the Florida Bar, which got the state to enforce the ban on unauthorized practice of law and got the courts to hand down a decision saying that she could type the forms but she wasn't allowed to converse with the applicants. She could only type what they wrote out, even if she knew it was a mistake. She has continued to try to conform with that; obviously, she hasn't been able to. So a Florida judge has recommended that she be put in jail for four months. For what? The unauthorized practice of law. Unauthorized? Unauthorized by whom? By the legal profession and by the law of the state. It's not incompetent practice. Nobody has said she has made a mistake. *Unauthorized* practice.

There are a number of solutions that might commend themselves in a neoliberal context. First, end the lawyers' monopoly. Introduce true competition in legal services. For starters, abolish the concept of the unauthorized practice. And permit non-misleading advertising.

Second, reduce people's dependence on lawyers. I suggest to you simplified divorce and probate laws so that people have the option to handle their legal problems by themselves. I suggest making the small claims courts available at times and places convenient to working people, and I suggest a way of making the collections by small claims courts enforceable. One of the great difficulties with small claims court might be resolved by a simple idea: make the renewal of any business license, like the renewal of auto licenses, dependent on that business having satisfied all outstanding small claims judgments against it — just as we refuse to renew auto licenses when there are tickets.

Third, institute genuine no-fault auto insurance.

Fourth, make the legal profession accountable to the public and not just to itself — by, for example, requiring a majority of lay people on the governing boards of every bar association and grievance panel.

I want to close by posing a question that neoliberals might ask. Would we accept putting a turnstile at the door of a courtroom? Every element of the justice system — the courts, the police, the prosecution — is freely available to everyone without regard to wealth, every element except one: access to the system through legal assistance. It turns out that justice is rationed according to ability to pay. Is that acceptable? Or should we make legal help available to everyone through a national legal service similar to the British National Health Service or through some scheme of national legal insurance similar to national health insurance? This may sound like a radical proposal but it merely satisfies the first commandment of the ABA's Ethical Code — that radical organization — which says, "A basic tenet of the professional responsibility of lawyers is that every person in our society should have ready access to the services of a lawyer." It is also a precept that we ask our children to recite every day in the Pledge of Alliance when we say "liberty and justice for all." I suggest that's a question that should be asked.

Justice Richard Neely: The reason courts don't work is that nobody wants them to work. Courts are a deliberately broken machine. If you take almost any government service—for example, the provision of interstate highways and waterways, schools, the provision of garbage collection or sewage, typical governmental functions— if those things don't work you can pretty well assume that either the people entrusted to do them are incompetent or enough money was not appropriated to get the job done. Because everybody basically wants his sewage collected and his water to flow and he wants fire protection.

That is not true with courts. Most people don't want court services, believe it or not. Everybody, for a different reason, doesn't want some piece of the court service that the government wants to provide. All of you who smoke marijuana and the few of you with enough money to use cocaine have absolutely no desire for those laws to be enforced. Almost everybody cheats on his income taxes. Let me quickly add that I don't, if you're an IRS agent. I can say these things because as a public figure I get audited all the time and I'm actually honest. But most people cheat on their income taxes in direct proportion to opportunity. The waitress doesn't report all of her tips. The doctor who takes in cash doesn't run it through his business account. Business executives deduct cars and airplanes and club dues. The guy who sells you the odd lot of wood in the wintertime and gets $75 doesn't report it.

There is an entire underclass out there who are members of a street culture—perhaps 15–20 percent of the population—who are involved either themselves or have children or relatives involved in nefarious activities of one kind or another. They do not want Rhadamanthine enforcement of the criminal laws.

Now, lots of people—most of us here, particularly white Anglo-Saxon Protestant upper-middle class folks—would like to have the criminal laws enforced. If, however, we also work for an insurance company, we are not a bit interested in having better civil law. The way we make money as insurance company executives is by keeping the court docket six years long so that we can take claimants who want $300,000 and diddle them down to a settlement of $35,000 on the grounds that "We'll give you $35,000 today or you've got a 50–50 shot at your $300,000 five years from now."

If you are an environmentalist, you do not want federal district courts or circuit courts of appeals, depending where your venue is, that can process administrative appeals quickly. You want the slowest, most broken down process possible because if you are against growth, it is the process itself that kills almost everything. If you are a storeowner and you get sued, you are against courts that quickly redistribute wealth. Nonetheless, you are much in favor of courts that will quickly collect your debts. If you are an impoverished tenant, your representatives will be very much in favor of courts that allow you to sue quickly for personal injuries, but you have absolutely no desire whatsoever to have a court that is efficient in evicting you from your dwelling when you fail to pay the rent.

So courts are largely providing a service that different people for different reasons don't want. It's like the government delivering to you every day three quarts of sauerkraut juice. You don't want sauerkraut juice.

What is there a consensus about? There is a consensus about violent crime—murder, rape, robbery, burglary, grand larceny, conceivably assault. There is also a consensus, generally speaking, about economic growth. We do not want projects—new schools, highways, other things—stopped because of incompetent courts. So you create institutions that only do those two things. And when you talk about the criminal law, if you expand the number of prosecutors, you've got to make sure that they only do murder, rape, armed robbery, etc., because otherwise they will start prosecuting you and me for election fraud, or for buying off foreign governments. We don't want that. So you tailor your institutions to make very sure that they focus on violent crime and not drug users.

Robert Nagel: Everyone knows the general contours of the criminal justice system. You have an elaborate set of procedures. You have complicated search and seizure laws that are enforced by the exclusionary rule. You have the warnings that have to be given to criminal defendants that are written out with great particularity and which are read verbatim by every police officer in the country. You have lengthy jury selection procedures. You have long and elaborate trials. You have lengthy appeal procedures.

That's what most people would tell you is the criminal justice system.

But, that is not the criminal justice system at all. That's what a few people get. Almost everybody else gets no procedural protections at all. What they do is plea bargain their cases; this whole lengthy trial procedure, for the most part, is applied to a very few or small percentage of the cases. The reason is that the procedures and the ideals that have gone into making those procedures have been so exaggerated that they are far too costly in human terms and in economic terms to be followed in most cases.

What the courts have done, I think, to the criminal justice system is that they have, in a rather wooden way, followed to zany extremes the logical implications of certain ideals. And it seems to me the criminal justice system and its defects are based primarily on the distrust of ordinary people. Most people don't understand why talking to a defendant politely is coercive, in the sense that courts frequently find it to be coercive. Most people probably don't understand why something like nude dancing is protected by the First Amendment. Why is that free speech? It seems odd to most people. There's a case today coming through the courts where the claim is being taken seriously that sleeping is a symbolic act of speech. Most people don't understand that. It's not intuitive.

I think this distrust is true of much of the criminal justice system and it's inherent in the way lawyers operate. They take ideas to their extreme. Legal explanations can make all of these things seem explicable to you. But the basic characteristic is that the legal explanations are foreign to ordinary people and are an affront to their common sense.

In fact, it seems to me that trying to achieve reform through lawsuits actually increases the grounds for distrusting ordinary people. The way lawsuits operate is to make ordinary people look worse than they are. For example, in a typical lawsuit what you try to do is make the other side look as bad as possible. If someone is trying to have a sensible law that might suppress pornography, what you do is color him as a person who really wants to suppress the Democratic Party someday.

So political positions become exaggerated and every possible ground for distrusting other people takes on legitimacy. And I think, in fact, political opposition does become uglier. People look worse when they're excluded from the political process, when they begin to feel that they have no opportunity to participate in or affect decisions that are important to their lives. The process becomes self-perpetuating. The use of judicial power makes people feel ugly, makes them feel as if they've been painted into a corner. They begin to act in extreme and ugly ways, and then the judiciary takes that as further evidence that they have to control social policy.

Mr. Kaus: I think the law is an area where you can draw some fairly substantive, clear distinctions between what I would say is the conventional liberal position and the neoliberal one. We all agree that necessary legal services should be provided to the poor at minimum cost, though not by lawyers if possible, and certainly not by a lawyers' monopoly—all the things that Philip Stern talked about. But there's sort of a strange schizophrenia in what I think is the traditional liberal position. Liberals start out trying to cut down on lawyers and litigation, and then they all end up going to law school and becoming poverty lawyers or constitutional lawyers—and they end up encouraging more litigation.

I think the basic divide between the liberal and neoliberal position is over whether you think litigation is a good way of resolving disputes, a good way of settling broad questions of social policy. I think it's a lousy way. So, whereas the sort of standard Ralph Nader position is that the poor don't get lawyers, we need access to the legal system for the poor, we need more lawyers to help the poor, I would say the neoliberal position is that lawsuits are wasteful and inefficient. We want fewer lawyers for *both* the poor and the rich. A national legal service or legal insurance which are often pushed by legal reformers would be a disaster. If you gave every person in the country the means to sue each other, we lawyers would easily beat the doctors and drain off 20, 30 percent of our GNP on lawsuits instead of the 10 percent that the doctors manage to get.

I do agree that we want to put some kind of a turnstile on the court system, such as user fees. We want people to realize that litigation is a lousy way to resolve things, that it's the last resort. If that means charging them money for it, as Justice Neely also recommended in his new book, we should do it. That's one clear difference.

The liberal position likes clinical law training. The neoliberal position says the most redeeming feature of clinical law training is that it may convince law students how boring the law really is so there will be fewer of them. The liberal position likes innovative law schools. Neoliberals want fewer law schools. Unfortunately, I think liberals, on the questions of broad social policy, have become addicted to using the courts to accomplish their ends. They've glamorized constitutional law. What liberal judges say is very similar to what Prime Minister Maurice Bishop of Grenada used to say. "We don't need these democratic mechanisms, these formal mechanisms of Westminster democracy. They really don't work very well. I can go out among the people and I'm really more democratic than having elections because I have direct contact with the people."

In effect, that is what liberal judges are saying. You have Abe Chayes at Harvard who says, "To think that Congress is representative of the people is to impose theory by brute force on fact." You have good liberals having contempt for the democratic process.

We want the criminal courts to worry about the violent crimes that really scare us and maybe lay off the drug users and bookies. By the same token, in sentencing, we want to distinguish between violent criminals who really should be locked away, and nonviolent criminals, with whom you can exercise the traditional liberal virtue of compassion.

Finally, I have doubts as to whether we're ever going to solve the crime problem within all the constitutional strictures that Professor Nagel talked about. If we really are concerned about crime, we should look at those instances where maybe the rights we have aren't worth what we pay for them in terms of increased crime.

There are two areas where there's room for heresy. One would be the Fifth Amendment right of self-incrimination. Lawyers have beat their brains out for 100 years trying to figure out just why you cannot put a defendant on the stand at a trial where there's no hint of torture and ask him, "What were you doing that night?" They ultimately have resorted to obscure Talmudic scholarship in talking about man's immortal soul, and when they start babbling about that, about the horror of people incriminating themselves, you know they're in trouble.

Let's think about whether we really want the full Fifth Amendment privilege. Of course, if you take away the Fifth Amendment privilege, a lot of the higher criminal justice system would change. The criminal suspect couldn't come into the station house and have his lawyer just say "shut up." The fact that the criminal suspect didn't come up with his alibi at that time could be held against him later in court. So you would have a substantial incentive to come up with some story. Then the police could go and check out the story and gain some leverage on the suspect's credibility. The entire *Miranda/Escobedo* rule would collapse. You wouldn't have to abolish the exclusionary rule. You'd be abolishing the substantive law that underlies the exclusionary rule.

The second point is the Eighth Amendment right to bail. I think that the average mugger on the street does not have a long time horizon. He doesn't worry about going to jail two years from now. A real deterrent would be if he has to go to jail tonight. Justice Neely favors a rule of *in flagrante delicti:* if you catch somebody in the act, he would automatically be denied bail. So at least there would be some possibility of not only severe punishment, but immediate punishment.

Michael Kinsley: Being without sin, it is my duty here to cast the first stone. I would like to just briefly bring you an anecdote from my own practice of law. In fact, this anecdote is the sum and substance of my practice of law.

My client was a small, neoliberal magazine published in Washington, and its editor, Charlie Peters, and we were being sued in small claims court by a freelance writer. Now the small claims court is really a model of some of the things neoliberals endorse. You don't need to have a lawyer there, usually. It emphasizes settlement of disputes. It looks for areas of agreement rather than litigation of disagreement. The procedures are very abrupt and straightforward. It's really everything a neoliberal should admire, so I didn't really think we'd have much problem.

I went into the court with Nick Lemann, who was the editor who committed the allegedly heinous sin in this case. We kept Charlie out in the lobby because we thought he looked too dignified; we were trying to look small and oppressed. And we saw a series of cases in which the judge would say "the purpose of small claims court is to make an earnest effort towards settlement," and he'd give a little speech about the need to avoid litigation that really could have appeared word for word in *The Washington Monthly.*

Then our turn came up, and the judge said to me, "Young man, have you made an earnest effort towards settlement?" And I said, "No, Your Honor"—this was under instructions from Charlie Peters—"we feel this is a matter of principle." And the judge turned beet red, and he said, "Young man! Small claims court is no place for principles!" He ordered us out into the hallway to settle with this freelance writer who was demanding $325; the judge told us to go settle for $82.

I went out and I told Charlie, "Look, we're just going to have to settle this case, I have to get back to work." And Charlie said, "I can't believe it. I can't believe it. I thought the courts were for justice." And I said, "Now, Charlie, small claims court is no place for justice." The only way I could get him to settle it was to agree to write him an article for free.

There is a small moral there: it is very easy to be contemptuous of the law, of lawyers, of justice, of courts, until you want something—and then even the staunchest neo-liberal suddenly wouldn't mind a little bit more procedure.

Question: Let me ask a non-legal question about lawyers. It seems to me that when we talk about why we have so many lawyers, one reason is that to a bright young person, the risk-to-reward ratio of law as against any other career is just unbelievably favorable, so they all become lawyers. How do we solve that problem? How do we make law a less attractive career?

Mr. Kinsley: One, increase competition or lower the opportunities to make income. As Robert Kaus pointed out, more clinical training will make people realize early on that there might be more interesting ways to make a living. One good thing President Reagan has done, incidentally, is reduce the opportunities to make a lot of money practicing law in Washington. But it takes a long time for those effects to work their way back—and the danger is that the hot shots and ambitious types go into investment banking, which is fruitless in an entirely different way.

Mr. Kaus: I think there are whole areas of law that can be done away with. Take administrative law in Washington. The Reagan administration has made a surprisingly effective start. Administrative law in Washington grew up around the creation of administrative agencies which were given sort of quasi-legislative powers, so instead of congressmen voting, you had lawyers debating. There's no reason for that and there are other fairly Draconian rules that you can come up with that are principles that will eliminate litigation.

Question: If I could make a point, I don't see any

black faces in this room. I don't know how many Hispanic faces there are in this room. I don't know what the socioeconomic background of the people in this room is. Yet it seems that part of the reason we're attacking these developments is that some of the people who haven't had access to the legal system are trying to find out how to use the legal system. I have yet to hear the members of the panel address this central question: What is the function of this legal system in protecting and balancing the rights of all parties within the overall fabric of American society?

Mr. Kinsley: One part of the neoliberal train of thought is that the rights of minorities, and civil rights of all sorts, and economic rights, are not best enforced through the courts. That has become in many ways a dead end, while succeeding in some ways. Certainly no neoliberal is against the Civil Rights Act, for example. But social justice is achieved through substantive measures like job creation. Giving poor people and minority groups lawyers and letting them come up with ever more ingenious ways to reinterpret the Constitution, to get the courts to force governments and companies to do things they don't want to do, is not going to work.

Mr. Kaus: One example is when I worked at the legal aid bureau at my law school. My job was to represent a woman whose house was being taken away from her. What was more helpful to that woman? That I as a lawyer would try to figure out a totally fallacious way in which she could keep her house which she, under the law, deserved to lose because she didn't have the money—or would it be better if that woman got a guaranteed annual income?

I think my position would tend to be that rather than giving the poor lawyers, what the poor really need is money that would help them avoid litigation. I was not good for that woman. That woman needed money, not a lawyer.

Too much of the energy of liberals has been devoted to giving that woman access to the courts, to bringing test cases and class actions. Too little has been devoted to the much harder task of convincing legislators to give that woman enough money so she doesn't need a lawyer and she doesn't need a class action. Let's have a jobs program, but not a jobs program for legal aid lawyers.

Question: I'm a politician and a lawyer in Maryland. I happen to agree that lawyers have been getting away with murder for a long time under the cover of doing something basically good. And this discussion in 1983 is one that should have been going on for decades in this country. But it is so terribly hard to discuss the legal system. One reason, I think, is the personal and financial interests of the people who have to make the decisions. The average state legislator makes $20,000 a year from his legislative salary and $20,000 from his law practice—and it's mostly probate, divorce, and real estate and auto accidents. So you're looking at economic ruin for the people who are supposed to discuss the issues. This is true in most of the legislative bodies, in all three levels of government. On top of that, the press hardly ever talks about it; academics rarely talk about the difficulty of discussing why the legal system is decades behind the rest of the government in modernizing, and gets away with such phenomenal theft, such phenomenal rewards for work that's not really needed.

Have you any thoughts of how to take this very sensitive subject and cope with it?

Mr. Kinsley: It's a very easy answer. Vote against the lawyers next time there's an election.

"During the (1982–83) academic year, 127,530 men and women were enrolled in law schools. These are among our ablest young people. If they had chosen productive work, they would have been on the cutting edge of the economic recovery we so desperately need. Instead, they spent the year sitting in some library, trying to focus their eyeballs on *Corpus Juris.*

" 'Anthropologists of the next century,' Michael Kinsley has observed, 'will look back in amazement at an arrangement whereby the most ambitious and brightest members of each generation were siphoned off the productive work force, trained to think like a lawyer, and put to work chasing one another around in circles.' "

— from "A Neoliberal's
Manifesto," The Washington
Monthly, May, 1983

"Court suits are increasing six times faster than the population; each year state courts alone report more than 13 million new civil cases. There are a number of reforms that would substantially curb our litigious ways:

MAKE THE LOSER PAY. Completely free access to the courts clogs the docket with frivolous disputes and causes lengthy delays that help the guilty escape full liability. And the expense of litigation deters many with valid claims— the angry consumer whose $300 refrigerator is defective finds it more expensive to hire an attorney than to simply buy a new refrigerator. . . . (So in some cases), make the loser pay the other side's legal fees. Lawyers who believe their client has a good case will press ahead; those who don't will be willing to settle, or won't take the case at all.

MAKE SETTLEMENT OFFERS COUNT. Good faith

efforts by one party to settle a case usually count for nothing if the other side insists on a trial. England has a better system: a party who refuses a settlement offer must fare better in court or be liable for the other side's attorney fees.

INCREASE THE USE OF ALTERNATIVE DISPUTE RESOLUTION. Arbitration and mediation aren't panaceas, but these techniques can be used far more to encourage early settlement. In European countries, for example, panels composed of landlords and tenants help mediate landlord-tenant disputes.

REFORM PROBATE. Ralph Nader has rightly called the current probate system the "screwing of the average corpse." Even the simplest estates in most states can't be probated without a lawyer, and in the 24 states that allow attorneys to charge a percentage of the total estate, it's not unusual for them to make $1,000 an hour for their toil. The system should be vastly simplified with a uniform probate code (now used in 13 states) that allows most wills to be executed without an attorney.

INSTITUTE GENUINE NO–FAULT AUTO INSURANCE. In most states, courts spend about 20 percent of their resources litigating injuries that arise from auto accidents. Yet the current tort system compensates the injured only if he can prove the fault of the other driver; as a result, nearly half the people seriously injured in car accidents receive absolutely nothing (from this process). Of every $1 motorists pay in insurance, only 44 cents goes to accident victims—the rest goes for overhead and attorney fees.

Far and away the nation's best no-fault law is in Michigan, where suits can be brought only in cases of "serious impairment of a bodily function, permanent serious disfigurement," or death. The quadriplegic can sue; the motorist complaining of vague back pain cannot. Insurance

premiums have risen more slowly in Michigan than nationwide, even though far more injured motorists receive
compensation."

—from "Breaking Out of the
Courtroom," *The Washington
Monthly*, June, 1983

BIBLIOGRAPHY

Articles in The Washington Monthly

Rowe, Jonathan, "Why Liberals Should Hate the Insanity Defense,"
    May, 1984
Smolla, Rod, "Self-Love and Libel," November, 1983
Hartman, Thomas, "Free the Law School 120,000!" June 1983
Neely, Richard, "Loser Pays Nothing: Why Our Courts are Overcrowded,"
    June, 1983
Nagel, Robert F., "How the Right Learned to Love Earl Warren," October,
    1982
Riedl, Hal, "Trial and Tribulation," July/August, 1982
Alter, Jonathan, "The Case for Selling Justice," December, 1981
O'Connor, Michol, "Inside a U.S. Attorney's Office," January, 1981
Kaus, Robert M., "Abolish the Fifth Amendment," December, 1980
Nagel, Robert F., "A Plague of Judges," November, 1980
Kaus, Robert M., "Strike it Rich for Socialism," July/August, 1980
Stern, Philip, "How to Bribe Judges, Fix Prices and Delay the Inevitable,"
    June, 1980
Kaus, Robert, "Power to the People: Making the Constitution Work
    Again," October, 1979
Kaus, Robert M., "How the Supreme Court Sabotaged Civil Service
    Reform," December, 1978
Kaus, Robert M., "The Constitution, the Press and the Rest of Us,"
    November, 1978
Bethell, Tom, "Freeing the Guilty," January, 1977

Jenkins, John A., "The Revolving Door Between Government and the Law Firms," January, 1977

Strick, Anne, "What's Wrong with the Adversary System: Paranoia, Hatred and Suspicion," January, 1977

Etzioni, Amitai, "No Place to Go," December, 1976

Bethell, Tom, "Criminals Belong in Jail," January, 1976

Peters, Charles and Kinsley, Michael, "Now You're Thinking Like A Lawyer," November, 1975

Forer, Judge Lois G., "View from the Bench: A Judge's Day," January, 1975

Peters, Charles, "The Screwing of the Average Man: How Your Lawyer Does It," February, 1974

Green, Mark, "The ABA: The Rhetoric has Changed but the Morality Lingers On," January, 1974

Fallows, James, "Death on the Road: Going Beyond Nader and *The Reader's Digest,*" December, 1973.

Graham, Donald, "Thinking for Ourselves: Questions We Can Start With," December, 1973

Toynbee, Polly, "Shooting Down Some Myths About Gun Control," December, 1973

Wren, Christopher, "Letting Rizzo Do the Thinking," December, 1973

Hoffman, Paul, "The Wall Street Lawyers in Washington," June, 1973

Books

Green, Mark, *The Other Government*

Hapgood, David, *The Screwing of the Average Man*

Neely, Richard, *Why Courts Don't Work*
            How Courts Govern America

Rodell, Fred, *Woe Unto Ye, Lawyers*

Stern, Philip, *Lawyers on Trial*

Stewart, James, *The Partners*

Woodward, Bob and Armstrong, Scott, *The Brethren: Inside the Supreme Court*

Health and the Environment

THE PANELISTS:

Phillip Keisling (moderator)
is an editor of
The Washington Monthly.
Bruce Babbitt is the governor of Arizona.
James Steinberg is a legislative assistant
for Senator Edward Kennedy
of Massachusetts.
Dr. Fitzhugh Mullan is the former
director of the National
Health Service Corps
and the author of
Vital Signs and
White Coat, Clenched Fist.
Dr. Robert N. Butler, the former
director of the National
Institute of Aging, is
currently head of the
geriatrics department at
Mt. Sinai Medical School
in New York City.
William Drayton, formerly an
assistant administrator
for the Environmental
Protection Agency, is
currently chairman of
Environmental Safety.

Phillip Keisling (moderator): Let me give you a little summary of what *The Washington Monthly* has said about health care over the years. On this issue, we're completely radical. Last year, we spent $322 billion on health care. That's almost 11 percent of the GNP, and twice the percentage it was just 20 years ago. At this rate, costs are going to go to $800 billion by the end of the decade. One interesting statistic: Last year, the average cost of health insurance paid by the auto companies added $600 to the price of an American car. At the risk of oversimplification, we're basically on the road to bankrupting ourselves to keep us well.

This has led the *Monthly* over the years to advocate something that I don't think is going to pass Congress next year. Draft the doctors, put them under a national health system, give them free schooling, tell them where they have to practice and in what specialty, and give them a generous salary—say $50,000 or $70,000 a year—but don't let them go fee-for-service. Basically, let's have a system that treats doctors like we do other life-protecting professionals like firefighters and police. The job they do is so important, the public has to control what they do.

This won't pass Congress tomorrow, obviously. In the meantime, I think it's important, not just to reduce costs that are clearly exorbitant,   but to try to change the values by which members of the profession operate. Let me give you an example of the problem. I had the occasion to fly to Nashville about a year ago and I sat next to a cardiologist. With much pride, he told me about how much he loved his work, how many hours he worked, and how fascinating the heart was as an organ. He truly loved it. But he also spoke with a lot of pride of how he had made $150,000 the year before—he was about 34 years old—and only paid $1,200 in income tax. He had a condo in Vail, and a Mercedes he wrote off as a business expense. At this very moment, he was on his way to Yellowstone for a fishing trip and was going to stop and talk to a friend about medical business and try to write it off.

The funny thing was, I asked him, "Would you do what you do for a third of the money?" He looked at me like he thought I'd just asked him whether he killed his patients deliberately. But he thought about it and he finally said, "Yeah, I would, because I love medicine and it's one of the most satisfying jobs that I ever had."

Governor Bruce Babbitt: The existing public health care system is going to drive us to bankruptcy unless we effect some radical changes. I'd like to outline our position in Arizona with respect to the two big ticket items: Medicaid, which is essentially a state-driven—although 50–50 federal/state-funded—indigent care program; and Medicare, which is, of course, relatively comprehensive medical care, without regard to need, for everyone over 65.

Medicaid can be described as a system in which the government says to an indigent person who is ill, "Go find a doctor, get the treatment, and tell the doctor to send the bill to the public." Now, doctors are human beings, and faced with the prospect of sending a bill to the public, human nature prevails. For that reason, we decided we ought to try some market economics. If we're going to provide for the indigent—Arizona was the only state that did not have a Medicaid program—why don't we design our approach along the same lines as procurement for construction, the building of schools, many other things. So we say we have 50,000 AFDC clients with the following demographic and actuarial characteristics, and we send the information out to the medical community and say, "Send

us a bid, we're going to give it to the low qualified bidder."
Radical stuff. We had unanimous opposition in the medical community; having become addicted to the prospects
of Medicaid, they opposed it.

But once those bids were out, human nature again
prevailed. Providers have sprung up, all kinds of community health care programs. The bidding is hot and heavy.
Through all of the bureaucratic noise and confusion, people
are getting care. They're getting good care by any compara-
tive Medicaid standard, and the state is getting it done at
real cost savings. Our Medicaid indigent medical care bill
went up less than 4 percent last year in the second year of
the program, a year in which medical costs nationwide
were escalating about 20 percent.

Emboldened by our success at the state level, we also
have a plan for Medicare, a radical plan. It's called needs
testing, modifying Medicare to make it available only to
those people who need it. If we're going to get entitlement
programs under control, we've got two basic ways to do it.
One is to start cutting back services. The other is having
the guts to send the services to only those folks who need
it. A radical idea.

The president is proposing to do it differently. The
president typically is saying we're going to institute for
Medicare at the national level co-payments and deduct-
ibles for everybody. Everybody is going to pay more. And
ultimately that means a regressive program which shuts
out poor people.

I would ask you to try this idea on Aunt Tessie, or your
father, or anybody else on the conservative side of the
spectrum who generally opposes government programs
except for the check in their mail. I construct a dialogue
with my father who lives in Sun City. My father is rea-
sonably well off. He's 85 years old. He believes that the

decline and fall of American civilization began with the election of Franklin D. Roosevelt in 1932. He has never admitted voting for a Democrat in his life. And I construct a dialogue about his Medicare reimbursement check in which I challenge my father, who complains about the decline and fall of America with progressive addiction to entitlements. People will listen.

James Steinberg: The subtitle of these five minutes is "Whatever happened to National Health Insurance?"

If we had been having this discussion 10 years ago, I think we all would be sitting here saying, "What should it look like?" Should it be a national health service or should it be some other kind of program to make sure that everyone is going to have health care? You will not hear the words "national health insurance" or "national health service" uttered within a 10-mile radius of Washington anymore. It is absolutely off the agenda.

Why did it happen? On the surface, there's even more reason for some kind of national health program than there was 10 years ago. The number of people who lack health insurance has grown. The amount of income that the elderly have to pay for health care beyond what Medicare covers has grown dramatically. The current recession has created 10 million additional Americans who don't have any health insurance at all. The burden has fallen on the states and local governments, who are trying to pick it up through public hospital programs and indigent care programs. It's getting harder and harder for them to do that.

Hospitals, particularly in cities and rural areas, are getting more financially strapped. Essentially, the cushion of good times is gone and it's harder to shift the cost of indigent care to private payers. Throughout the system, you hear the screams of crisis. And yet nobody talks about the need for comprehensive reform.

Of course, some people are taking matters into their own hands. In Massachusetts, we have just seen what has got to be the strangest alliance of people to put together a very, very regulatory cost containment system. The principal motivating factor was the Massachusetts Business Roundtable. The presidents of the largest corporations in the state got together and said, "We can't stand this anymore, we cannot compete, our businesses are going under, our premiums have gone up 70 percent in four years from Blue Cross." And they said, "We're not waiting for government, we're not waiting for anybody."

But there are costs when business gets tougher. It used to be that if a hospital had 20 percent charity care, they'd load that cost on to the Blue Cross premium and, in effect, business and employees, working people, were subsidizing that cost. It was a nice cushion because it allowed you to do some things and not get really caught with people being put out in the street. More and more you're seeing that those cushions are gone.

A major reason for the situation is the effective efforts of those interest groups which have decided that reform is not in their interest. It's interesting that when Medicare was first proposed, most of the institutional interests — the AMA, American Hospital Association — were radically opposed. If you were to propose taking away Medicare now, they would be the first to scream. But those groups have been remarkably effective.

In 1978, President Carter made his big push for the cost containment program. At that time, health care costs were rising at a rate about two and a half times as fast as the overall rate of inflation. The American Hospital Association got nervous. In the one year following the introduction of the cost containment program, they instituted a thing called the "voluntary effort." Dramatically, hospital costs dropped to the point where hospital costs were actually slightly lower than the consumer price index. That year Congress was persuaded by the American Hospital Association to kill cost containment and, as will come as no surprise to anyone, the following year, hospital costs were once again two and a half times the CPI.

The kinds of crises that Governor Babbitt was talking about are only going to get worse. By 1988 or 1989, Medicare will be bankrupt, and Congress will have to do something about that, and it has the kinds of choices that Governor Babbitt was talking about, which is either to significantly cut benefits, which is essentially the Reagan administration approach; raise taxes, which no one thinks is a plausible solution; or else engage is some kind of systematic reform.

Dr. Fitzhugh Mullan: The one piece that Phil left out of *The Washington Monthly*/Charlie Peters formulation for a National Health Service, was, as I recall, that every doctor get a Jaguar. That was to keep them quiet, to cut out the kvetch factor. If they complained, give them a Jaguar, give them $20,000–$30,000 a year and then that's it. I was a little skeptical up to that point; I heard about the Jag and I was ready to sign up.

The issues, as I see them, can be reduced in a perhaps oversimplified form. We have a fixation on technology as the answer to our medical problems which quite conveniently fits the needs of the profession. I say the profession in the expanded sense, not just the physicians, but the medical suppliers, the drug industry, and so forth, which both produces high tech and lives off the very considerable proceeds.

Allied to that, however, is the belief of the citizenry in high tech. You only need to follow the liver transplant craze of the moment and the fascination with the 11 p.m. news of how Baby So-and-So is doing in Pittsburgh to see how riveted the public is on this. Secondly, there's a kind of social complacency. The profession is used to being well treated by the public and the public is used to treating the profession well and paying them well. And I think those assumptions need to be challenged.

I am a believer in a national health service. I had the privilege of running a program called The National Health Service Corps, working in it first as a field physician and then later as its director. It still exists in a rather embattled condition in the present administration. I lived in the hope that one day we would drop Corps off the end and it would simply become The National Health Service. That direction is clearly not the one in which the country and the administration has moved.

I am battered from that experience. I grew up in medicine hearing and even saying to myself, well, it's only a matter of a few years, in the next congressional election, we will have national health insurance. And we have moved drastically away from that in the present environment. One well-known reason is that the profession does not believe in those innovations. The public—and I don't mean to get the monkey off the back of we physicians—also has been led to believe that these innovations are expensive, or un-American. If the problem was only turning around and, as with the air traffic controllers, firing all the doctors and raising up another generation, that would be one thing. But the problem is that the body politic in America does not yet seem to have the focused and sophisticated understanding that it needs to take the medical system in beneficial directions.

I have a more modest and specific package of proposals that I'm calling "An Agenda for Primary Care."

The term has been coined to serve as ballast to the

sub-specialty drift that took place in the '50s and '60s. The components that should make up a primary care strategy or agenda are the following. One is that the preponderance of physicians trained in this country should be trained as, and practice as, primary care physicians, and we should cut out the drift to neurosurgery, to thorasic surgery, to pediatric nephrology. We have quite sufficient backlogs of talent in those areas. Seventy percent of physicians should be trained and incentives should be developed to keep them in primary care.

Two, you've got to have equity in reimbursement. The sicker a patient is, the more a doctor gets paid in our system. If a patient is anesthetized or if a patient is there for radiologic procedures, the doctor gets a lot. If the doctor really has to talk to the patient, as in primary care, the doctor gets less. That's a system which serves certain doctors, but does not serve the primary care strategy, and it doesn't serve patients.

Third item. There should be a one percent factor in primary care, a federal factor. That is, one percent of the physicians in the nation should be available at all times to be used as a national health service corps, as an Indian health service, as an emergency medical relief, as an epidemiologic intelligence service, as a variety of forms. That speaks at the present time to about 4,000 physicians. We have only about 1,000 now in the National Health Service Corps.

Fourth, there ought to be a National Institute of Primary Care that serves as a research and new knowledge base for the whole primary care movement.

Fifth, and a very important idea: we should have an International Health Service Corps. The Cubans have developed a blueprint for us. They have done marvelous, effective—some would argue sinister, though I would not—but extremely effective things with a small cadre of physicians specifically trained for work abroad. The linkage of that international component with the idealism and principles of many people—and particularly young people—and the benefits that would come for the nation in terms of what the Peace Corps has done, and what the Cubans clearly have done for themselves in a foreign policy way, would be very important.

Sixth. Finally, there's a concept—community oriented primary care—which speaks to consumerism and democracy in the way that health care is administered and practiced and that should be the glue that sticks this whole primary care strategy together.

Dr. Robert N. Butler: We're beginning to approach the threshold of consideration of the longevity factor in American life and politics. Let me begin with a few key imperatives. First, the body of knowledge has become so powerful now that the opportunity to actually intervene in the retardation of the aging process is at hand. We have already seen dramatic drops—a 30 percent drop in deaths from heart disease and stroke in the last decade, not alone as a consequence of gerontology.

Another feature is demographic. We are in the midst of a longevity revolution. I've called it the century of old age. What was once the privilege of the few has really become the fate of the many. The United Nations World Assembly on Aging in the summer of 1982 revealed a doubling of the number of persons over 60 throughout the world by the year 2000. And 60 percent of those people over 60 will be residing in the Third World.

We were a Third World country once, too. In 1830, only one out of every three newborn babies survived into their 60s. Now 80 percent of newborn babies live out a full life. We've gained, in average life expectancy since the year 1900, 26 years—almost equal to what was gained in average life expectancy from the Bronze Age, 3000 B.C., to the year 1900.

We've reached a watershed of enormous proportions. The fastest growing age group in the United States is the 85-plus age group. And there has not been one change in the inherent natural life span. We're only talking about increasing survivorship within an inherent span that appears to be between 100 and 110.

Another aspect of the demographic issue as it bears upon the longevity factor in politics and national life is that it's a women's issue. Women outlive men and that increase is becoming increasingly more marked. Eighty percent of the people in nursing homes are women. So one of the political realities that we're going to be confronted with is a need to be much more responsive to the lives of women and older women.

We also better understand the meaning of health costs. There's been a shift in the age of morbidity and mortality. The cold breath of morbidity and mortality is now associated with old age; 80 percent of deaths occur after 60. Little wonder that health costs now occur in old age. There's also been a general inflation since 1965. The health industry's inflation is the result of an enormous amount of inefficiency, waste, fraud and abuse. But, also, hospital workers for the first time have begun to get decent pay. They were never covered under the National Labor Relations Board because they were largely women and minorities. And much of our health care bill is actually residential—for example, the nursing home industry whose cost last year hit a shocking $27 billion.

What do we do from here? Clearly we have to develop some policies. I don't know about overplanning, but I do know that no sector of American society—church, foundations, government—is effectively responding to, or even deeply thinking about, the aging population that's in front of us. And I suggest we can't wait until the baby boomers reach the golden pond to begin to do a little bit of prudent effort. For example, you can't suddenly declare war on senility in the year 2011. You can't suddenly decide that we're going to have an adequate cadre of geriatricians in the year 2011. You can't suddenly deal with the nursing home issue in 2011. And 2011 is the first year that the baby boomers—born in 1946 and afterwards—turn 65. By 2020 to 2030, 20 percent of our population, by current projections, will be over 65.

Let me offer an agenda of action, though I clearly can't be more than superficial. We need an R&D effort that takes a percentage of that Medicare budget and really wrestles with the issue of Alzheimer's disease, which is the most predominant form of senility. The nursing home is the iron lung of geriatrics. Once we've begun to make some progress with regard to senility, we will significantly empty our nursing homes.

Second, there has to be major educational reforms in medical school. It's unacceptable that you can graduate without having stepped a foot in nursing homes. There are now more patients in nursing homes than in hospitals—1.5 million people.

We must begin to confront the issues of corporate medicine—the "McDonaldization" of nursing homes and hospitals—and the extent to which that's going to lead, and already has, to cream-skimming of the healthier and better-paying patients. We must introduce some real reimbursement reforms. We're beginning to do that a little bit with the Reagan administration's diagnosis related groups (DRGs) that started on October 1 in 46 states, which means a prospective cap on Medicare payments instead of retrospective payment. But I'm not aware of there being an eleventh commandment on that tablet that Moses brought down from the mountain that says the present fee structure for doctors has to remain what it is. I agree with Dr. Mullan that it's absolutely essential that we get away from the organ-by-organ, procedure-by-procedure payment system, where those who are involved in comprehensive primary care get paid the least. It's time for a major renegotiation with already existent dollars.

There also needs to be a fundamental movement towards a solution of the issue of long-term care and the nursing home situation. I've sat on task forces for the Carter administration and the Reagan administration. No one can really move. It's time for a major private/public long-term care commission. We've been involved in some behind-the-scenes discussions along that line, to begin to look at things like private nursing home insurance. We're not being effective in thinking about the realities of the type of security the people want. There aren't many things that people fear more than growing old, losing their mind, and being put away. We could also begin to think about some real taxes on tobacco and alcohol, which obviously have a lot to do with the kind of wretchedness we often see in the later years.

I'll conclude by saying that we're embracing, I fear, all too easily a kind of ideological politics of austerity. It's always been true of the things that are scarce. But I submit that perhaps more scarce than anything else is imagination, coming up with a practical, rational use of resources and a rational distribution of those resources in an egalitarian manner.

Technology, in my judgment, has been wonderful. Imagine for a moment, Robert Koch and Louis Pasteur sitting down with President Teddy Roosevelt in 1900, with a bunch of demographers and epidemiologists sitting at the table. Imagine that one of them said, "You know, there's this crazy guy, Paul Erlich, who's come up with a concept of the magic bullet, an antibiotic; there's a fellow who's got an antiserum for diphtheria; there are possible ways of reducing the deaths of mothers giving birth to children. But we *can't afford old people*"—that was a cover story in *Forbes Magazine* not so long ago, incidentally—"because we now have an average age of 47. If we move ahead with this degree of progress, we may hit an average life expectancy of 73 just 70 or 80 years from now."

Fortunately, there were no nay sayers in the year 1900. We have, I think, had a considerable triumph of survivorship. And my guess is that in the long run it will be the yea sayers and the positive, affirmative, imaginative policy makers who will make a tremendous difference as we face the extraordinary population of aging, not only in this country but the entire world.

William Drayton: We were talking about older people just now. I'll just quickly mention that we're now having another demographic change of fundamental importance among older people. Next year the average educational attainment of persons over 65 will be 50 percent higher than in 1974. That has very major political implications. It's the passing of lower class older generations to middle class older generations. We know, from studies of older people, [with higher incomes,] that they live longer and have less illness. So a lot of things are mixed together.

Now with the environment, it's hard to quantify because we're still so ignorant. But it's probably—at least in the long-term, maybe the medium term—the most cost effective and humane way of lowering the costs of the medical system. Every year there is more and more toxic pollution because the elements of the economy that produce those by-products are among the faster growing. Since there's never any more air, land, or water, and since it takes a very long time for the human body to adjust to new substances, that means the problem gets worse every year.

By the early 1970s, the public had sensed this and forced action. The Congress later responded with a quite historic wave of legislation from the last year of the Ford administration, 1976, through 1980. In 1976, the Preventative Hazardous Wastes Law was passed. It basically said that the 40 to 200 million tons of hazardous wastes this society generates every year, depending on your definition, is no longer going to be disposed of randomly around the countryside — 85–90 percent, according to the best surveys, unsafely. We were going to try and make sure this waste goes through licensed safe facilities. We also said we were going to investigate all the chemicals in commerce and all the new chemicals to see whether they were safe. At that point, we didn't have a clue how many chemicals we were producing. It turns out there are about 55,000. We learned that after the first census in 1978.

In 1977, we saw revisions of the air and the water and the drinking water laws to control toxics as well as conventional pollutants, and even a modification of the pesticide law to make it actually practical to control pesticides. The next several years were devoted to some of the most basic research and standard-setting. The early '80s, these several years right now, is the time when all this was supposed to be actually implemented. And using EPA's own data — I'm focusing on the EPA at the moment — that literally doubles the amount of work to be done.

Unfortunately, we had a political change in 1981 with a rather different agenda. And taking the EPA case, Mr. Reagan came in with a proposal to cut EPA's budget by two-thirds, after inflation is considered. His program of the mass staff firings by his eighteenth month of office — had Doonesbury not stopped him — would have resulted in only 200–300 out of the 5,300 people at EPA headquarters still sitting at the same desks. Fortunately, there was a Congress and Doonesbury, et al., so we "only" have had a

30 percent cut and no resources for any of the new programs.

I'll just give you a sense of what some of that means in practice. Who is enforcing the hazardous waste law against 120,000 firms that are under regulation for the first time? Well, there are 75 people. Now, efficiency is great, but that's hard. We've actually investigated and taken regulatory action in the last three years against 20 pesticides—out of the 40,000 used in commerce. Going back to the hazardous wastes program, GAO reported just a week ago that we've actually managed to issue permits to 24 in the last three years—that's eight a year—of the 8,000 active hazardous waste sites in the country. If you have one of these things near you, you face the prospect of waiting 500 years, if you're an average case, to find out whether it's a safe facility.

Voluntary compliance, which any regulatory program has to depend on, is being demolished. Companies simply can't count on their competitors complying. When you go from 98 percent voluntary compliance, which is what EPA used to have, to 96 percent, you have twice as many people out of compliance, and everyone else is dragging their feet a bit more. One industry which produces cyanide heavy metals and all sorts of other lovely things, has had an 85 percent drop in its orders for pollution control equipment.

No one has been realistic about the resources. In the era of general penury, we have had this historic wave of promises, and no one has been willing to face up to paying the bill. The Carter budget was in real terms flat for the last three years, though it went up significantly in the first year. OMB is too weak politically and otherwise to be able to reallocate resources from relatively fat agencies to relatively strapped ones. Mr. Reagan deserves no further comment.

One last point. Analysis of the polls show that this issue is as potentially powerful as the crime issue was in the early '70s. There is almost nothing that people fear as much, and can control as little, as toxics in the work place and in the environment. It is an almost universal concern, and the intensity factor is extraordinary. A single issue analysis that Lou Harris did last fall showed that traditional environmental issues had a net swing of 11 percent. This much more intense issue of toxics is probably 15 percent. So for every 10–15 percent of the population that goes into the voting booth, this one issue can change their minds.

"We tell others in the business of protecting our lives — soldiers, sailors, policemen, firemen — where to serve. The policemen can't all patrol Park Avenue. The sailors all can't be based in San Francisco. Just because an Army officer wants to be a cavalryman is not an adequate reason for letting him be one. We do not permit even the greatest general to charge us whatever he wants. Is there any logical reason why medical salaries, specialties, and places of work should not be equally subject to public control?

The public should take over the entire cost of physician training — we already pay a high percentage — and it should give every intern and resident a generous salary plus a free Jaguar. This arrangement would deprive them of the last shred of justification for the self-pity that seems to possess all but the most decent doctors in later life, the self-pity that says because I was strapped to pay those tuition bills and because I was exploited as an intern and resident, I am now justified in robbing my patients blind. The doctor who thinks $75,000 a year is his divine right — indeed, a bare minimum from which to advance to ever

greater fiscal heights — is the spiritual father of our present
health delivery system."

> —from "A Radical Cure for High
> Medical Costs," by Charles Peters, in
> *Newsweek,* May 28, 1977

BIBLIOGRAPHY

Articles in The Washington Monthly

Cummins, Ken, "The Cigarette Makers: How They Get Away With
Murder," April, 1984

Keisling, Phillip, "Protection from Catastrophe: The Medicare Reform
We Really Need," November, 1983

Keisling, Phillip, "Radical Surgery: Draft the Doctors," February, 1983

Cohen, Toby, "Accidents Will Happen," February, 1983

Riordan, Teresa, "The Wards Are Paved with Gold," February, 1983

Piasecki, Bruce, "Beyond Dumping: The Surprising Solution to the
Love Canal Problem," January, 1983

Madlin, Nancy, "Lead Astray: How the EPA Let One Get Away," October,
1982

Goldberg, Paul, "Muzzling the Watchdog," December, 1981

O'Donnell, Frank, "Manager of the Year," December, 1981

Braham, Dr. Robert and Lee, Dr. Thomas, "The Worst Care Money Can
Buy," June, 1981

Frankel, Glenn, "The Tragedy of TOSCA: Chemical Poisoning the EPA
Can't Control," July/August, 1979

Lemann, Nicholas, "Let the Nurses Do It," April, 1979

Babyak, Blythe, "Califano's Cigarette Campaign: All Smoke and No
Fire," July/August, 1978

Lee, Thomas H., "Thinking Like a Doctor: Why They Charge So
Much," April, 1978

Toynbee, Polly, "Socialized Medicine: One Patient's Story," November,
1977

Kurtz, Howie, "The Real Problem with the FDA," July/August, 1977

Glasser, Ronald J., "A Real Cause of Cancer," October, 1976

Hapgood, David, "What People Like You and Me Are Doing to Get Better Health Care," October, 1976

Peters, Charles, "A Revolutionary Answer to Medical Costs," October, 1976

Thiemann, David, "Why the Ambulance Comes Too Late," October, 1976

Fallows, James, "The Cigarette Scandal," February, 1976

Mendelson, Mary A., "The Screwing of the Average Man: Where It All Ends," January, 1974

Blumenthal, David and Fallows, James, "The Care We Need and Want," October, 1973

Ignatius, David, "The Morality of Medicine," October, 1973

Books

Anderson, Peggy, *Nurse*
Butler, Robert, *Why Survive? Being Old in America*
Klaw, Spencer, *The Great American Medical Show*
Mullan, Fitzhugh, *White Coat, Clenched Fist*
Starr, Paul, *The Social Transformation of American Medicine*
Toynbee, Polly, *Hospital*

Values

THE PANELISTS:

Nicholas Lemann is a national correspondent for *The Atlantic* and the author of *Out of the Forties.*
James David Barber is the James B. Duke Professor of Political Science at Duke University and the author of *The Presidential Character* and *The Pulse of Politics.*
Hendrik Hertzberg is editor of *The New Republic* and was President Jimmy Carter's chief speechwriter.
Amitai Etzioni is University Professor at George Washington University and author of *An Immodest Agenda.*
Daniel Yankelovich is head of the research firm Yankelovich, Skelly and White and the author of *New Rules.*
Deborah Fallows is a linguist and is

currently writing a book
about motherhood.
Kathleen Kennedy Townsend is an
attorney for the
Governor's Anti-Crime
Council in Massachusetts.

Nicholas Lemann (Moderator): I want to start by
quoting part of a political speech:

"It is impossible to capture in words the splendor of
this vast continent which God has granted as our portion
of his creation. There are no words to express the extraordinary strength and character of this breed of people
we call Americans. Everywhere we've met thousands of
Democrats, Independents, and Republicans from all economic conditions and walks of life, bound together in that
community of shared values—family, work, neighborhood,
peace, and freedom. They are the kind of men and women
Tom Paine had in mind when he wrote during the darkest
days of the American Revolution, 'We have it in our power
to begin the world all over again.' "

Does that sound familiar to anybody? That was Ronald
Reagan's acceptance speech at the 1980 Republican
convention.

Now let me quote Jimmy Carter, the same year, at the
Democratic convention:

"I want teachers eager to explain what a civilization
really is. I want women free to pursue without limit
the full life of what they want for themselves. I want
our farmers secure in the knowledge that the family
farm will thrive with a fair return on the work they do.
I want workers to see meaning in the labor they perform. I want people in business free to pursue with

boldness and freedom their new ideas." And so on.

Some of you may be wondering what in the world we mean by the word "values," and I would begin to define it at its most practical and political level. I think one reason Ronald Reagan is president is that he was able to use a rhetoric of values in his 1980 campaign and Jimmy Carter wasn't. To me this was particularly dramatic because Carter himself was elected in 1976 using a rhetoric of values. In his acceptance speech that year, the same man who in 1980 ran through the litany of gently phrased assurances to interest groups that I just finished reading, said:

"Business, labor, agriculture, education, science, and government should not struggle in isolation from one another but should strive toward mutual goals and shared opportunities. The poor, the weak, the aged, the afflicted must be treated with respect and compassion and with love. I have spoken many times about love but love must be aggressively translated into simple justice." And on and on in that vein.

One of the questions we'll address in this panel is what happened to this guy? It seems plain to me that those who want to see a liberal in the White House ought to be thinking hard about why it was that in 1980 the leader of the Democratic party could not talk about values, and that the leader of the Republican party could.

Of course, liberals don't have much trouble talking about values where they pertain to the activities of government. The conservative mind is deeply suspicious of statements like, "Government should be compassionate." The liberal mind has no trouble with that and, in fact, embraces it. But liberals are—and I think this is especially true since 1970—very reluctant to talk about personal values. God was, I believe, not mentioned once in Carter's 1980 acceptance speech. Reagan, as you remember, ended his speech very dramatically, saying, "I'm afraid not to end this with a moment of silent prayer," which brought down the house.

The Carter administration, you may also remember, had a conference on the family which—does anybody remember that?—was a festival of relativism under whose guidelines even a fraternity house officially qualified as a family.

There are good reasons Democrats feel uncomfortable talking about personal values. Liberals are acutely aware of the arrogant, exclusionary possibilities contained in confident talk about patriotism, the nuclear family, and religion—a sense that those who don't fit the program are going to be written off. To some extent the Democratic party is made up of people who, over history, have been written off under what was the current definition of American values. But the fact is that during the 1970s, the conservative movement was becoming increasingly comfortable and adept at talking about personal values, with results at the polls.

Now let's get to a deeper and more complicated level. I think there's another reason liberals began to become less and less comfortable talking about, and even thinking in terms of, personal values. There began to be a gulf—or more precisely, a non-relationship—between their political beliefs and their personal values.

A fairly broad liberal political agenda was in place by the late Forties which by 1975 had been substantially achieved. During the Forties, Fifties, and early Sixties, the rhetoric of liberalism was full of references to personal sacrifice and to putting yourself on the line. The roots of this meeting on neoliberalism are directly in the Kennedy Peace Corps, which had that kind of passion and feeling at its very core. The question was, what were you going to do in service of what you believed?

That this question was seriously asked and seriously answered gave liberalism a moral force. It gave liberals an ability in their best moments to speak with the conviction and authority that people have when they have decided not only what they think, but also how they are prepared to live as a result. As liberals won the great battles of Medicare, civil rights, food stamps, and aid to higher education; as liberals got effective control of both Houses of Congress; and as liberal judges came to dominate the nation's courts, what had started as liberal causes became liberal institutions.

This had a huge effect on the culture of liberalism, especially since its moment of institutional triumph coincided with a major recession which turned people's attention more toward making a living. It also coincided with the movement that everybody, including half of our panel, has coined terms for—the "culture of narcissism," the "me-decade," the "self-fulfillment culture," "national malaise." Liberals started to make more money—and they could make more money as liberals. (I think all of us wince when we see those stories in the paper about the saintly doctor in the ghetto who billed Medicaid for $2 million last year.) And with the agenda largely achieved, the ties between a liberal's beliefs and his career also became looser.

So a new and very prevalent image of liberals gained force. Speaking as someone who doesn't live in Washington, it is an image I think is prevalent outside of Washington. Liberalism now was headquartered in Washington. It was affluent, it was unpatriotic, it was collectively dedicated to maintenance of the status quo. It trusted courts and regulatory agencies more than it trusted the wisdom of the people. It was no longer intensely eager for firsthand experience with the areas of poverty and prejudice that were at the heart of its concerns. It had lost the habit of hard thought and the habit of willingness to undergo personal sacrifice.

Yes, this image is exaggerated. Yes, everyone on the right, from neo to far, dines out on it excessively. But honestly, I don't think we can say that it's without truth.

What I hope we address in this panel is first, how liberals should talk about values and second—more complicated and I think more important—how liberals should live their lives.

James David Barber: Back when I lived in West Virginia my mother used to take me as a child to Marmet, where they had the polio hospital—they called it "infantile paralysis" in those days—for children. You came into the room and saw rows of iron lungs lined up along the hospital floor. Each iron lung had a little person inside with his or her neck sticking through, with a mirror up in front that they often decorated with stickers, pipe cleaners, and things of that sort. And I thought one of the most touching details was that the girls had their heads on a pillow and they would comb and fix their hair so they could see it in the mirror. It was an experience that I'll never forget, but an experience which, thanks be to God, is behind us. And thanks also, of course, to technology. We can now go from one end of the Kanawha Valley to the other without ever seeing a polio hospital.

It seems to me that we can take some courage from the apparent changes in values that we've seen in our own lives. There is a wisdom in the reception to the humor of Mr. Watt and Mr. Reagan with respect to cripples and loin cloths and so forth. The reception shows that their humor is a kind of regression of about 20 years. As a result of the civil rights movement, the women's movement, all the way back to the mental health movement, there really have been some sea changes in our society. There is a sense of the respect for the individual that I think is new. Ask a black person how it is now to travel through the South. It's different. It's not the same kind of country that we lived in 50 years ago.

Liberalism or neoliberalism as well is a mixture of

compassion and realism. It's not a soapy-headed idealistic business; it's in accordance with human nature. What we need to do is concentrate, at least initially before complexity sets in, on the simplicity of it all. If I have a worry about it, it is that neoliberalism will succumb to the intellectual embroidery—as they say, beware of complicated reasoning that leads to cruel conclusions.

The compassion that's needed, I think, grows out of our heritage. We just simply won't put up with a government that punishes the most vulnerable people in the society—children and the poor. We should insist that we get past all of the complicated ways in which we are trying to manipulate those people into prosperity by giving them a form of money, namely food stamps; a form of credit, let's say Medicare; a form of subsidy in housing—everything except what makes a difference between poverty and prosperity, and that's money. Of course, if you gave the poor money there might be some people who would sit under the banana trees and laugh at the rest of us. I think that would be fine. Every society needs a saving remnant of mockers at the obsessions that it exemplifies. You need some hippies sitting back there just thinking it's funny as hell that all of these people are going to these offices all day.

Finally, we need to infuse that process with some realism. We're moving into an era now, I think, of the fictionalization of American politics, a period in which we are much more fascinated with the gesture and the posture and the symbol than we are with the empirical reality upon which democracy rests. Reagan provides so many sterling examples of this, one of which I'll conclude with.

Reagan used to tell the anecdote about how racial integration came to the Armed Services, and that was because at Pearl Harbor there was a black sailor who cradled in his arms a machine gun and shot down the Zeroes with it. He got a medal, and that's how integration came to the Armed Services—after Pearl Harbor. A reporter finally got up the courage to challenge Mr. Reagan on that and said, you know, the story wasn't quite like that. There was a lot of segregation in the Armed Services, down to Harry Truman and a certain executive order. Now what was Reagan's response? I quote: "I remember it very well. It was a very powerful scene."

So I hope that neoliberalism becomes, not just another posture or gesture, but as you see and have seen in *The Washington Monthly,* a movement which is led forward across the fields of fact.

Hendrik Hertzberg: The Carter administration, to classify it ideologically, was not, strictly speaking or even loosely speaking, a liberal administration. There's never been a liberal administration in this century. Maybe the last one was the Madison administration. I mean "liberal" in the sense of an administration led by the recognized leader of the liberal wing of the Democratic party, a liberal in the sense that the Reagan administration is conservative.

The Carter administration was certainly not conservative, and it was certainly not neoconservative. By a process of elimination—and also because of the presence high in the counsels of government of people like James Fallows and Walter Shapiro, and because the only subscriber in south Georgia to *The Washington Monthly* was a peanut farmer from Plains—we have to conclude that Jimmy Carter was America's first neoliberal president. So his experience does have some relevance for this gathering.

Jimmy Carter was elected on values, on moral values. When he talked about a government that was as nice and competent and compassionate and as full of love and as good as the American people, he was talking about those values. Those values had been trampled on and scorned and dismissed as unrealistic by the people who enthusiastically brought us Vietnam and Watergate and the use of the FBI to try to force Martin Luther King to commit suicide.

Some of the policies of the Carter administration were direct reflections of the values he articulated in the campaign. At home, policies like support for civil rights, for universal voter registration, for amnesty for Vietnam war resisters; and abroad, policies like carrying to fruition the Panama Canal treaties, and of course support for human rights. And most of all, maybe even more than human rights, was what might be called Carter's tempered Christian passivism, reflected in his pursuit of nuclear arms control and in what I would call his conscientious refusal to use armed force except where it followed the failure of all peaceful alternatives and was done in a manner proportional to the task. And the only example of that, of course, is the Iran rescue mission.

As the rescue mission showed, there was often a gap between intention and performance. Part of the problem was Carter's own reluctance to call on the wells of feeling that he had tapped during the campaign. Despite all the talk about love in the campaign, he was reluctant to get corny. He saw rhetoric as being manipulative in a reprehensible kind of way.

I tried for a couple of years to get Carter to adopt a slogan for his administration, not because I think that slogans *per se* are a good idea, but because I thought he needed one to help people understand that there was some moral coherence to his way of governing. His administration wasn't any less coherent than FDR's or Lyndon Johnson's or John F. Kennedy's. They pulled their act together with a slogan which made their set of programs seem coherent.

The first slogan I tried to sell to him was "The Beloved

Community," believe it or not. I thought this was a great idea. People would talk about Beloved Community programs; we'd have gone from the New Deal to the Fair Deal to the Great Society to the Beloved Community. And it was an idea that came from where Carter came from, a phrase that comes out of the civil rights movement and the black church, one often used by Martin Luther King. They used it to describe both the movement for social change, the people making up the movement, and the goal of social change. So it seemed to fit in nicely. We dropped it into the end of the 1978 State of the Union speech, but it failed to attract any notice, partly because we didn't do any backgrounding on it, and partly because it was just too soft a slogan for him to adopt a year into his presidency.

When Carter did lose touch with his connection to moral values in his presidency, he lost everything. And that's what happened in 1979 as he got bogged down in technical minutiae and dull foreign policy issues like foreign trade, and as the gas lines began to grow. His last great attempt to recapture the magic, to get back in touch with the wells of feeling about moral values that he had succeeded with in the campaign, was the malaise episode, and I just want to talk for a minute about that.

If you remember, it happened when Carter cancelled yet another energy speech, went up to Camp David quite unexpectedly, and improvised this extraordinary drama of public soul searching and consultation. Then he came down and in a dramatic speech, of which the principal authors were Jimmy Carter and Pat Cadell, announced to the country that it was in the grip of a crisis of confidence. He never used the word "malaise," by the way. The speech had three parts. It started with an admission of his own inadequacies put in the words of others, then he outlined this crisis of confidence, and then he called on the country to recapture its confidence, beginning with an attack on the energy problem.

That whole episode is now generally recalled as a catastrophe, and it turned out to be. But I hope it's not too self-serving and parochial of me to point out that the speech itself was a stunning success. It was the most successful presidential speech in history since the advent of television—measured by such yardsticks as the immediate jump in the polls and the volume of favorable mail. The day after that speech Carter went on the road and was received with an enthusiasm that he had never been received with before, even during the campaign. People responded because they recognized that what he said about a crisis of confidence in the country and losing touch with the moral values we've been talking about was true. He touched that nerve again.

Two days later, when there was a kind of a Jonestown of the cabinet, the firing of the cabinet, it all fell apart. Having diagnosed the patient's moral neurosis, Dr. Carter was unable to provide the cure. He'd raised expectations so high that when he proved unequal to the task of meeting those expectations the public took a terrible revenge. And in that disconnection lay the final failure of the administration.

It's taken for granted now, of course, that the Carter administration was a failure, though it could be argued that there was nothing wrong with it that couldn't have been cured by a couple of good helicopters. But I recognize in more honest moments that that's an alibi. It was a failure. And one of the reasons was the failure to make the connection between moral impulses and political actions. That connection is called ideology, and the Carter administration didn't have one. Or, more precisely, Jimmy Carter had a moral ideology, but not a political ideology. He had moral impulses but not a model of the political power of relations in society that would build those moral impulses permanently into the process of government. The creation of an ideology is what the liberal side of the political spectrum desperately needs. That's what the conservative side has. That's what this meeting is all about, and why the creation of a neoliberal alternative is an honorable task.

Amitai Etzioni: When we talk about a neoliberal platform we ought to have some positive things to say, things we stand for and not only things we stand against. This is difficult for us to do; as responsible, thinking people, when it comes to personal social values we are deeply divided against one another. When it comes to the question of what to do about the family, for example, there's usually an embarrassed silence in such meetings. And when it's broken, it breaks into a violent conflict. When we talk about pornography, soon we are torn between libertarian notions and traditional liberal notions. It's very difficult for us to come together.

After quite considerable effort I did stumble upon two values which I think we can share. One is the value of mutuality, of caring, of acknowledging the value of deep, lasting commitment to other people, especially one on one. The second value I'll call civility. You could talk about community—beloved, if you wish. That basically suggests, in some divergence with the popular interpretation of Adam Smith but not at all in conflict with what he has written, that we need to learn to balance self-interest with a commitment to the commons. If everybody goes to the forest and fells a tree, pretty soon the hillsides will be denuded and then we'll say we need to have a government program to make sure that as everybody takes down a tree, somebody also plants a seed. The only alternative to coercion is a voluntary commitment to community.

Where do these positions divide us from other groups? On the one side, we have, first of all, the libertarians.

Maybe they get just one percent of the vote, but they have a surprisingly large following on the campus and elsewhere—a kind of intellectual fashion of sorts. And if you read the libertarian platform carefully, it has an interesting attribute. It doesn't recognize community at all. There are only two bases—the individual, who is enshrined, and government, which is to be hated. There's nothing in between. So when the libertarians call, for instance, for the demolition of Social Security as a government activity, they do not suggest that we should take care of one another. They just retreat to everybody doing what's right in their own mind.

Then we have the Chicago school of economics, which these days is applying its immoral principles to the total fabric of human relationships. So, for instance, Gary Becker studies marriage as a transaction that basically works like this: Every evening before you turn in you tally up the losses and gains for the day. If the gains exceed the losses, you stay for one more night. And if the balance is negative, you take to the door.

The notion that all relationships are utilitarian exchanges, that you should watch out for number one, is completely incompatible with all we know about what makes a community function.

Just as we have the individualistic extreme—the libertarian, the pop psychologist, the laissez-faire economist—we also have the Moral Majority and the new authoritarianism. The essence of their message really is that community is so dear that you must suppress the individual in order for the community to thrive. They want to legislate prayer and they want to legislate banning of abortion and they want to legislate death penalties—all things that do not allow choice.

The question is not whether there is room for self; the justice lies in seeking a balance. And I agree very much with Betty Friedan that this does not mean accepting injustice and racism and sexism. Institutions need to be destroyed in order to liberate those who have suffered for centuries. But that does not complete the process. The second stage is necessary, to build a new balance of relationships in which men and women and black and white and all others will find their rightful place.

Daniel Yankelovich: I would like to elaborate on the point that Nick Lemann started with, particularly with respect to young people. Many young people may espouse liberal values on issues like South Africa, the military, women's rights, but they don't do very much to carry them out. They don't march, they don't go to Mississippi, they don't lick envelopes or volunteer to help out. It's the kind of liberalism at no personal cost, a decadent form in that sense. There is a lack of moral force that derives from the huge gulf between professed beliefs and the way we actually live. In the vulgar but vivid phrase, people aren't putting their money where their mouth is.

There are several reasons why this is the case. One of them is a hangover from the 1960s, when there was an extraordinarily naive division of effort between privileged youth and the establishment. The role of privileged youth was to point out what was wrong; the role of adults was to fix it. One of my associates, Lawrence Skelly, refers to it as "Look, there's a wart." The presumption was that one's moral obligation was completed by pointing to the warts. Somehow this generation that rejected their parents presupposed that their parents would fix things. And the parents, in their dumb way, accepted that peculiar division of effort.

There's a more fundamental cause which has to do with the internal contradictions between the ethos of liberalism and the social climate of today. I'm not referring to the me generation of the '70s but to the next phase of that in the context of the '80s. To oversimplify, the current social climate encourages the individual to look out for himself or herself, and to win. The emphasis is on individual choice. It's on one's own, though it extends the self just a tiny bit to one's own ethnic group or union or locality. It stresses a lot of competition. You see this fierce competition between states and cities and ethnic groups and classes and everybody else. And there's an enormous emphasis on strategy rather than on principle. It's smart to be pragmatic, to cheat on your taxes, to brag about it even when you don't do it. To scramble, to come to the very edge of legality. And I think there's a feature that is, as people are, both appealing and ugly. There's an adventure and excitement to playing the game to win it. It is not the game for its own sake; it is the game to win.

This climate is not going to change. In fact, the country is just beginning to rev itself up along these lines to compete more effectively against Japan and West Germany. It needs the energy that's released in this way, and it's going to be released in a variety of forms. The emphasis on the pragmatism and on the winning and on all those elements is going to be a very strong part of the climate. Unless the contradictions between the unexamined liberal ethos and this social climate are resolved, young people will either simply discard their liberal values as they get a few years older in favor of those underlying values that conflict with them, or else they'll give them lip service while they live another way of life.

I think it's very important that there be, at least initially, in reconstructing liberalism a focus on newer issues that don't carry the burden of liberal ideology from the past. A few issues suggest themselves along those lines. One is the whole idea of jobs—both improving people's involvement in their jobs as the core of an industrial policy, and job creation. There are all of the environmental issues that revolve around toxic waste and the like; reversing the arms race without picking up all of the baggage of the peace movement. Another theme that young people especially would be very responsive to is to stress our obligation to the future, which is so terribly neglected. By definition it's these young people's own future you're talking about. On issues like Social Security, every one of them feels they're going to be done out of theirs. On the nuclear arms race it's their own survival. On child care, it's their children.

Another theme would be a stress on winning through improving quality: quality of the job, quality of the products we make, quality of the schooling we get, quality of life for all persons, quality of our relationship to other people — the quality of civility and mutuality, if you will. We can stress the fairness of giving everybody a chance to compete in the race with the tools they need. People accept that stress today on competition rather than cooperation. Another theme is to stress compassion for those who fall behind, which is not the same thing as the legal emphasis on the rights of the losers, which is, in itself, a losing issue in today's climate.

We have to do more to make it possible for young people to actually play the game of politics with all the values that they believe in of challenge, excitement, show biz. I wouldn't downgrade the symbolism of the "great scene" aspect because it's almost necessary for that engagement. It's part of the times in which we live. The point, from a strategic point of view, is to find a way to build an approach to issues that integrates the kinds of values that Amitai Etzioni was talking about with the kind of values that are part of the social climate of our time.

Deborah Fallows: Like most women, I notice every day the things that the women's movement has made a lot easier for me than they were for my own mother: an education and the array of professions that are available, ears sometimes for my opinions. But I've also noticed how the women's movement has seemed to define its goals for women, telling them that success should be measured just like men have always done it—in terms of power and jobs and money, and that you can throw in managing the children, keeping the house, and maintaining the household help as well.

This view is unnecessarily strict and narrow; it is also an unimaginative prescription for a modern liberated woman. There are many women who have taken the essential message of the women's movement to heart—the message that it's a woman's right to pursue her own dreams, and the need to take responsibility for the course of her own life—and yet who are moving out in a very different direction. It's a direction that focuses, at least for a certain period in their lives, on family and especially on children. They believe simply that there's nothing more important than raising children and making a family. There's no reason to think that the essential feminist ideals should be incompatible with these beliefs. Yet most women who share them feel that they've been excluded from the ranks of liberated women.

Those who are looking for guidance in matters of family and children, and who are searching for support in their decisions about work and family, are hearing only from the right. The political effects of the women's movement has been to leave these issues in a vacuum for the right to move into. They moved into it precisely because these issues hit such a deep chord for individuals and for our society. It's something that we all feel matters very much.

I don't mean to write a formula for families in the strict Norman Rockwell sense. Rather, I'm talking about family to mean living in a certain way that requires of people some common qualities. It means long-term commitment to partners whom we choose, and for a lot of people that means thinking about someone besides yourself for the first time in your life. It's a commitment, often, to children, which is even greater; they can't take responsibility for themselves and they can't take care of themselves. You may choose to have children but you can't choose the children you get. You get who's born to you and with that you accept the risks of their health and personality and intelligence, and you're committed to loving them.

A second quality that comes with families is an enforced need to care for other people. That means to act many times during each day with those people and their welfare in mind. It may mean acting at your own expense. But as anyone who has spent time with children recognizes, their sense of stability and of being loved become the foundation of their behavior as adults.

All of these things fall ouside our standard system of compensation and reward. We ask things of our families that we wouldn't dare ask of anybody else. We give to them in terms in which no compensation, especially monetary compensation, makes any sense at all. Not all families are perfect, clearly, and not all family members adopt these virtues just by being a member of a family. But on the whole, the more society acknowledges and seeks these family values, the better in certain respects it will be. The more understanding it has of those who are dependent and in need, the more responsible it will be to provide for people—the poor, the young, and the old—who cannot provide for themselves.

Women don't need to forfeit their progress toward independence and self-sufficiency and equality by paying attention to families and children. The women's movement needs to recapture some kind of pride in working for

family and children, and it needs to admit and champion
the worthiness of doing that.

Finally, it must be recognized that families and children are no longer the domain of only women. The women's
movement encourages men to participate, in the sense of
pulling the load, doing their share. But I think women
would do better to stress instead what men are missing
with families and children. That's something the women's
movement is only going to do after women really believe it
themselves.

Kathleen Kennedy Townsend: The real question before
us is not just what to think, but how to act and how to
develop the character that gives us the courage to look
clearly at our problems and do what's necessary to solve
them. We're here today because we've realized that many of
the solutions that were proposed 20 years ago are no longer
working. We're still stuck very much with the problems of
poverty and racism, of sexism and of crime. The question
is, how are we going to get beyond the automatic responses
that some of us have had to these problems?

It seems to me that we've discounted two ways in which
we can start to rethink those problems. One is religion,
and the second is voluntarism.

There's been a great reaction to the Moral Majority
because they brought up the subject of religion. There is a
sense among many liberals that this is an inappropriate
subject for political debate. I've seen a similar reaction to
the subject of voluntarism, as though it's inappropriate to
urge people to take a little time out of their lives to actually do something to help people.

This doesn't make sense to me. If we look historically,
religion and voluntarism have been a great boon to the
causes of the left, through the abolitionist movement,

through Jane Addams and the settlement houses, and especially with the civil rights movement.

Two experiences I've had seem to illustrate the problem. I'm now working on the Massachusetts Governor's Anti-Crime Council, and working with an idea to start an ROTC program for police officers. We now have about one-sixth as many policemen per violent crime as we did 30 years ago, and this primarily affects those who live in the inner cities. The purpose of the program is to vastly increase the number of police. So I talked to a police union member about this and he said, "Well, Kathleen, I think it's a great idea. It would increase the number of police, it promotes the idea of service, and as a citizen I'd support it 100 percent. But I'm a member of the union and I'm going to have to fight you on it." This seemed incredible to me—could we have imagined 20 years ago that a policeman would have to wear two hats, one as a citizen and one as a policeman?

The second story involved a friend who is in Legal Services. We've heard that Legal Services might not provide the best care for the poor. But it certainly helps when people are being evicted from their homes, or when their food stamps are cut unfairly. A friend of mine who worked for Legal Services, and then had a baby, decided that she would still like to work two afternoons a week. She realized she couldn't get paid for that, so she offered to go back to her old job as a volunteer. She was told that wouldn't be possible.

What Martin Luther King taught during the civil rights movement was that you're not going to change the world's social conditions simply by legislation. You first have to affect people's hearts if you think anything will endure. So he made a moral appeal to people. He also realized, and I think a number of other people realized this, that the courage to act in ways that are sometimes not in your self-interest comes through habit and through experience with actually seeing what is wrong. Volunteering, helping somebody else, will help give us that kind of courage, and will give us the experience to see what is, in fact wrong — not just what we've learned through reading books or attending conferences.

"The Moral Majority is on to something. It's on to it too narrowly; it has applied its definition of virtue specifically to particular political positions that are insensitive to the discriminations suffered by blacks and that are militaristic and anti-female. This has given the idea of moral virtue a bad name. But the basic feeling that a spiritual renewal and a repairing of American moral fabric have something to do with each other is not far off the mark. These New Right groups may have a simplistic, reactionary, even dangerous view of moral values, but at least they understand the importance of the subject. Most liberal Democrats nowadays do not appreciate its importance. Discussion of moral values makes them uneasy."

"In 1968 my father, Robert Kennedy, was able to earn the trust of black and white women and men largely because it was clear that he believed in them and in their values. His religious conviction made him acceptable to many working people who after his death could vote only for George Wallace. At the same time, many blacks felt they could trust him. On his return from South Africa in 1966 he wrote an article for *Look* magazine entitled "Suppose God is Black." The title struck at all those who believed in God but were still unwilling to treat blacks as equals or to welcome them into their neighborhoods, schools, factories, offices, and boardrooms.

"My father appealed to both rich and poor, black and white, because he took religion seriously.... Knowing of the love and admiration many liberals felt for my father, I've never been able to understand why liberals don't comprehend the power of a moral appeal and why they don't begin to take religion seriously, too."

—Kathleen Kennedy
Townsend, from "A Rebirth
of Virtue: Religion and
Liberal Renewal," *The
Washington Monthly*,
February, 1982

"In the National Organization for Women's infamous 1971 resolution on voluntarism—which current NOW leaders would happily forget—women were urged to volunteer only for social change and feminist groups, and not in community service where their labor was exploited (they should get jobs for which they could get real pay and real professional credit instead) and where the officers and boards were usually composed exclusively or mostly of men. I myself never liked that stand on voluntarism . . . That polarization between feminism and voluntarism, as a matter of principle, was as false . . . as the seeming repudiation of family."

—Betty Friedan, from *The
Second Stage*, Summit Books,
1981

BIBLIOGRAPHY

Articles in The Washington Monthly

Noah, Timothy, "The Big Massage," February, 1984
Lemann, Nicholas, "Values, Personal Choice, and the Failures of Liberalism," December, 1983
Townsend, Kathleen Kennedy, "The Forgotten Virtue of Voluntarism," October, 1983
Lemann, Nicholas, "Community Without Conformity," September, 1983
Townsend, Kathleen Kennedy, "A Rebirth of Virtue: Religion and Liberal Renewal," February, 1982
Fallows, Deborah, "Why Mothers Should Stay at Home," January, 1982
Lemann, Nicholas, "The New Patriotism," January, 1982
Shapiro, Walter, "Madeleine Lee, Meet Nancy Reagan," March, 1981
Slater, Philip, "Getting Off the Money Standard," March, 1980
Easterbrook, Gregg, "Fear of Success," February, 1980
Fallows, James, "Who's a Snob and Who's Not," June, 1979
Lemann, Nicholas, "Why Warnke Quit," May, 1979
Kaus, Robert M., "What's Wrong with Roots," March, 1979
Levine, Arthur, "Serving the Rich: The Washington Y," December, 1978
Peters, Charles, "The Solution: A Rebirth of Patriotism," October, 1978
Baldwin, Deborah, "Motherhood and the Liberated Woman," July/August, 1978
Lemann, Nicholas, "The Halstonization of America," July/August, 1978
Lemann, Nicholas, "When Bluegrass is Better than Ballet," February, 1978
Massey, Thomas, "The American Class System and How to End It," February, 1978
Wilkes, Joseph, "How to Stop Masturbating," October, 1977
Lemann, Nicholas, "Success in America," July/August, 1977
Lemann, Nicholas, "From World War II to Clay Felker: How America Bought its Way to Happiness," March, 1977
Lemann, Nicholas, "Going Home," November, 1976
Bethell, Tom, "Prisoners of Liberation," September, 1976
Fairlie, Henry, "The Spoiled Child," November, 1975
Fallows, James, "What Did You Do In the Class War, Daddy?" October, 1975
Shapiro, Walter, "The Liberal Plot to Kill God," October, 1975

Rothchild, John, "American Communes: Voluntary Maoism," June, 1975

Shapiro, Walter, "What Politicians Really Want," April, 1975

Lessard, Suzannah, "Taste, Class and Mary Tyler Moore," March, 1975

Peters, Charles, "The Zero Defect System," July/August, 1974

Fallows, James, "'Making It' Revisited: Nader, Podhoretz, and Morris," July/August, 1973

Lessard, Suzannah, "Civility, Community, Humor: The Conservatism We Need," July/August, 1973

Lessard, Suzannah, "The Ms. Click, The Decter Anguish, the Vilar Vulgarity," January, 1973

Branch, Taylor, "Prisoners of War, Prisoners of Peace," August, 1972

Lessard, Suzannah, "Aborting a Fetus: The Legal Right, The Personal Choice," August, 1972

Lessard, Suzannah, "Let Those Hillbillies Go Get Shot," April, 1972

Lessard, Suzannah, "America's Time Traps: The Youth Cult, The Work Prison, The Emptiness of Age," February, 1971

Books

Barber, James David, *The Pulse of Politics*

Etzioni, Amitai, *An Immodest Agenda*

Friedan, Betty, *The Second Stage*

Janowitz, Morris, *The Reconstruction of Patriotism*

Yankelovich, Daniel, *New Rules*

National Security

THE PANELISTS:

Jonathan Alter (moderator) is an associate editor of *Newsweek.*
Ernest Hollings is a Senator from South Carolina.
Dina Rasor is director of the Project on Military Procurement.
Andrew Cockburn is the author of *The Threat: Inside the Soviet Military Machine.*
Earl C. Ravenal, a member of the Libertarian party, is a professor of International Relations at Georgetown University.
Paul Savage, chairman of the political science department at St. Anselm's College, is a former Lieutenant Colonel in the Army and co-author, with Richard Gabriel, of *Crisis in Command.*
James Fallows is the Washington Editor of *The Atlantic* and author of *National Defense.*

J onathan Alter (moderator): For people who may
be a little bit confused about what people mean when they
use the term "neoliberalism," I think the defense debate
offers a clearer example than most. Generally, neoliberals
like to challenge the faulty or outdated assumptions held
by both the left and the right. In defense, those assumptions were particularly sterile, I think, until the last few
years. The right endorsed an approach which suggested
that the liberal solution to social problems in the '60s—
i.e., tossing money at problems—was a legitimate way of
approaching defense. On the left—and I don't think this is
an oversimplification—the legitimate hatred of war and
the destructive power of weapons led to an unwillingness
on the part of most liberals to learn the details about
military policy. By doing so, liberals essentially left themselves out of the debate over defense policy in the last 15 or
20 years.

Senator Ernest Hollings: I'll try to approach the problem of national security in a budgetary sense. As president,
I would call in the heads of the various departments and
have them list their requirements. And if the Secretary of
the Army listed these items—an M-1 tank, an infantry
vehicle, M-16 rifle ammunition, uniforms, what have
you—you'd program that cost with the proper outlay rate
and the proper inflation rate over a five-year period. Then
you'd take the Navy and all the ships, the Secretary of the
Air Force with his missiles and planes, and the Marine
Corps, and you'd look over to the righthand side at your
bottom-line, five-year projected figure. And you'd realize
immediately there's just not that much money in the world,
literally.

We've done this in the Senate Budget Committee. You

jump from a B-17 in World War II at a cost of $97,000, which still shocks me, to a B-1 model that costs $410 million for one plane. You just cannot afford all that you want. So you'd go to your Secretary of the Navy and say, instead of a 3½-ocean Navy, you'd have a 2½. Or more particularly, with respect to some of the missions, you could try to economize, looking up at the Greenland, Iceland, United Kingdom—what we call the GIUK gap—and say, rather than a task force of a carrier with 100 planes that costs $20 billion, you could land-base 200 planes in the United Kingdom itself at a cost of $7 billion and take care of that particular mission. You'd look at other missions that have been assigned. The Air Force has the A-7 and the Army has the AH-64 helicopter. Only one is needed, and when you look at both of those you wonder whether either one is effective. But you'd approach it from a mission standpoint and then move immediately into your procurement practices.

I found some years back, looking at a promotional list of 69 generals in the Army, only one in procurement. And I learned if you are really gung-ho or a good officer you were given a brigade or a field command or sent to Korea or to Europe. The dunderbuns end up in the procurement end and by the time they get there after about 25 or 30 years of service, they only have two years left. Where can I, after retirement, get me another little job? Oh, yes, this contract that I'm supervising. There's an incestuous nature, and that must be cured. We must try to attract the talent into the procurement end so we won't spend 17 years to obtain an M-1 tank.

Then you'd move, after all of those particular changes were made, to the actual need. Over-prepared for nuclear war, we are under-prepared for conventional warfare. You can do away right readily with an MX missile or B-1 bomber, or a *Divad* (anti-aircraft gun), and save billions. A great portion of it should go to try to reduce this deficit, but some of the savings should go to fleshing out our conventional readiness—operation, maintenance, flying hours, steaming hours, rapid deployment force, more F-15s, F-16s, attack submarines.

You'd go then, of course, to the matter of the overall percentage that we increased this budget, and I have opted for three percent. You might say that's just a political position taken by a candidate for president who has always been gung-ho for defense. I tried to hold onto a consensus that we had for defense at the beginning of the Reagan term. I met just the other day with Charlie Duncan, who used to be the Deputy Secretary of Defense, and I was relating to him the figures of what we had really done since he'd left town. I said, "You know, we increased the defense budget in 1981 over 1980 some $37 billion; 1982 over 1981 $34 billion, and then this last December, the '83 budget, $30 billion—or $101 billion in three years." He said, "Senator, there's no way in God's world to spend $100 billion. I've run the Pentagon and I know its procedures intimately and there's no way to do it." We've just run amok.

More than a demonstration of military power, we need a demonstration of will power. And that's where the draft comes in. I debated this all-volunteer army some 10 years ago. At that time, the casualty figure showed that the war in Vietnam was being fought by the black, the poor, the disadvantaged. I responded at the time that that's what we'd end up with—an army of the black, the poor, the disadvantaged. My civil rights friends are all running around looking for an issue. They don't have to avoid this one. If you were the president, you would want to call on a cross section of your society. A nation calling upon the least advantaged in our society for its defenses is a dangerous anachronism. You wouldn't have any troops in Lebanon this afternoon if there was a draft. I can tell you that right now. We wouldn't be even debating it. You'd be awfully, awfully careful about your military commitments and allocations.

Dina Rasor: There is a group of people inside the Pentagon who want to do the right thing and would if they thought they could get away with it. They cannot, and they get tired, as Ernie Fitzgerald characterized it, of setting their hair on fire for one brief week of glory as a whistle-blower and paying for it with the rest of their life and their career. So three years ago, a group of them came to me and asked me to set up a front—there's just no other word for it—so they could feed me unclassified documents about what's going wrong in the Pentagon—memos, test results, audits, whatever. I would put them together, as a journalist, try to sort out any bias, and then work with the press.

We are not political. I've walked a very narrow and straight line the last few years, not being left or right. I will not deal in foreign policy. I do not talk about the morality of war and peace, something, by the way, that I've been flailed upon by liberals and libertarians for. I think the left and the right talk about defense like it's either you smoke or you don't smoke, and it's either/or. Either you should smoke or you shouldn't smoke. I liken it more like going onto a diet. You have to have a little bit of food to sustain you, but the tendency to binge is always there.

When these people first came to me, I thought they were nuts. I really did. But they really know the system. For example, I was astounded to find out that the Pentagon cheats on their weapons testing. I guess I was being naive. But they cheat in a big way. The people who develop the weapons are also the people who test the weapons. Senator

David Pryor of Arkansas said it the best. It's as if you allow
a student to make up the test, take the test, and then grade
himself.

Not surprisingly, all these weapons systems are coming
out with A's and A+'s.

I discovered this cheating first with the M-1 tank in its
second operational test. The tank had, in the second operational test, 1,007 maintenance actions. Every time the tank
broke down, they'd write up a maintenance action. The
tank would break down once every 16 miles. Well, it's safe
to assume some of these are going to be changing light
bulbs, the stuff that does not threaten the tank and its
mission. But when they saw this 1,007 maintenance actions—
and when they realized they had to reach a goal of 90 miles
between failures—the Army put together what they call a
"scoring conference." (They've now changed the name of it
because it's gotten such a bad reputation.) This is a group
of officials sitting around, and it's kind of like magic. They
look and say, "Well, that's not really a failure. The mechanic
had a hangover that day, so O.K., let's throw that out." So
they took those 1,007 maintenance actions and threw all of
them out except for 171. Lo and behold, the tank went 92
miles between failures—and they declared it was a success.

I went with my sources and we went back to the tests. To
show you there are honest people out there in the Pentagon,
there was an honest test director. He sat there scoring the
tank out on the field. Every time that it had a failure that
he thought was serious enough to damage the mission of
the tank, he would write it down and grade them. And it
ended up the tank went 34 miles between failures.

When this came out publicly, the Army just came
unglued. They claimed the M-1 was getting better in the
third operational test—what I call the "prosperity is just
around the corner" line. And we hear that all the time—if
you've ever sat through any congressional hearings, you

know another $1 billion and we're going to have the best state-of-the-art tank.

Then we found that the tank, scored in the same way through the third operational test, only went 43 miles between failures. By this time, they were saying it was going 295. On the first operational test, they had even thrown out nine catastrophic engine failures as not counting. The Army said I didn't understand their detailed analysis of how you do the failures.

What it finally comes down to is just common sense. A soldier isn't going to care what caused that catastrophic engine failure in his tank when he's in the battlefield. He's not going to care if it's the fault of the mechanic. In any case, he's going to be a sitting duck and most likely killed.

Paul Savage: Well, we're all very happy with liberalism here. And it rather reminds me of the Academy Awards, an orgy of self-congratulation. There's a darker side to liberalism. First of all, I'd like to remind you and your class that the people that rigged the laws that sent 55,000 men to their deaths in Vietnam were the upper middle class and the middle class—and they were mostly liberals. They sent the blacks and the poor instead. You're the kind that sent them there. And you're doing it again with the volunteer Army.

But to the Army. The Army is quintessentially liberal. When it is paternal, solicitious of its men, organized, disciplined—this is liberalism, very much so. The trouble is that the Army, during Vietnam, took on not the characteristics of liberalism, but the characteristics of what American society really is—careerism, individualism, utter disregard for the concern of your men, me first, officers serving six months in combat, enlisted men a year. In time, the Army became ridden with drugs, fraggings, mutinies, desertions—thousands of them. We produced

800,000 heroin users in Vietnam. And by the way, the junk was flown in by CIA subsidiary aircraft.

That being the case, you now have an Army which reflects the society which you are. It is civil in its values. It is no longer professional. It turns over at the rate of 85 percent per year. Army Training Reports found in 1979 that no unit which turns over 20 percent per quarter — irrespective of money, training or discipline — could ever be combat ready. So you have an Army that has done what you wanted it to do — to be civilianized, to reflect civil morality and values as they are.

A proper Army would indeed be a "liberal" army, probably on the Israeli or Prussian model. But this would be, of course, unacceptable to the sensibilities of humanistic liberals of the middle class, because it would have to have your sons serve by conscription and you won't bite that bullet. The consequence, I suggest, within about 10 years, will be a staggering military catastrophe.

Now, something on the positive side. I had a surprising call a couple of months ago. Where Dina Rasor has attacked their mechanicals, myself and my colleague, Richard Gabriel, have attacked their souls. They're very sensitive about that. I got a call from the Deputy Chief of Staff of Personnel of the United States Army, General Elton, and we had a meeting. They moved the entire top personnel staff out of the Pentagon, and we met at the conference center at Fort Belvoir. There were about six generals, all the top brass in personnel administration, and about 30 colonels. We met from 8 in the morning until 6 at night, and moved through every one of the issues I've just covered — careerism, excessive staffing, ineffectiveness, the inability of the Army to institutionalize excellence, the inability to test effectiveness against efficiency — it's not the same thing — quality of soldiers, how to lead them. So they are, in a sense, beginning to look in at their souls, and they're not seeing a very pretty sight. It's something of an administrative cesspit, in my judgment.

To give the Army credit, it has looked at itself and it's frightened. So I think with a bit of push from the outside and some encouragement to look at themselves from the inside, there is a possibility of a self-reformation on the Prussian model of 1815, which probably produced the world's most effective army in two wars.

Andrew Cockburn: A few days after the infamous downing of the Korean airliner, I was on a TV show with Richard Viguerie and William F. Buckley. The moderator, Ted Koppel, asked what I thought the incident showed about Soviet military power. I said it shows their incompetence. It took them 2½ hours to find this plane. They'd been looking for it all night and kept missing it, and it showed they were extremely rigid and bureaucratic since they obviously didn't have the flexibility to figure out if they had an order to shoot down planes in their air space. In a way, it gave a rather rosy view of our chances against Soviet air defenses. And Messrs. Viguerie and Buckley erupted in fury and said, there I was, a bloody liberal making excuses for the Russians, again. Which I thought was a very choice example of the "threat inflation" mindset.

At the core of threat inflation is the assumption that the Russian military isn't like any other large bureaucracy. Most of the time we're told what a huge and cumbersome bureaucracy they have. Yet the Soviet military is not seen as a huge bureaucracy, behaving like bureaucracies do with feuding and fighting, pursuing their own internal concerns as opposed to their external purposes. We're told that the Russians always produce the right weapon for the right purpose, that their military is an organic monolith where the chaps at the top make decisions and then everyone immediately marches in step and carries them out. So that if they shoot down a Korean airliner with 269 people on board, that is because Mr. Andropov, closeted with his closest aides, decided that's what they were going to do. The idea that actually it might have been a gigantic screw-up—that's not allowed. Because once you started making the Soviets actually like anyone else in this regard—for instance, like the Pentagon—you start to get into trouble and you have to look around for other reasons to justify the $322.5 billion defense budget.

I'll give you some examples of the way their attempts to make themselves into a super-efficient "totalitarian" organization come unstuck. My favorite is something called the "vertical stroke." To keep everyone up to scratch, you make—and this exists in the U.S. military as well—every commander at every level absolutely responsible for what goes on in his command. If you're a regimental commander, for instance, and Sgt. Yenkelshi gets drunk and slugs another sergeant, then the sergeant gets into trouble, his company commander gets into trouble, his battalion commander gets into trouble, and so on. So you think "jolly good"— the commanders make sure nothing happens in their command. Wrong. What happens, of course, is that the sergeants still get drunk and slug each other, but the regimental commander, not wishing to have a black mark on his record and get transferred to the Chinese frontier, covers it up.

Like the Pentagon but in a different way, there's also an inability to cancel a weapons system. We have the classic story of the MiG-25 fighter plane. The MiG design bureau got its development contract because the Americans were building the B-70, a very high altitude, supersonic bomber. Then the Americans played dirty and cancelled the B-70 bomber. That didn't matter too much because the MiG-25 just carried on. Then the Americans heard the Russians were building this wonderful new fighter. The wonderful new fighter the Americans had at that time was the F-4, so of course, the wonderful new fighter the Russians were meant to be developing looked curiously like the F-4 in all the American artists' impressions of the Russian plane. Come 1967, the Russians unveiled the MiG-25 at an air show and it looked, of course, nothing like the F-4 at all.

But that was no problem, either. Look, the Americans said. The Russians have done something brilliant. This aircraft can fly at over three times the speed of sound, it's got an amazing range, so what we need is something to deal with it. All of which did wonders for the development program of the F-15. Disaster struck in 1976 when Lt. Belenko defected and flew a MiG-25 to Japan. The Americans found to their consternation that it was actually an old clunker made of steel and vacuum tube electronics. It could stay in the air for a maximum of 28 minutes and the pilots were expressly forbidden on pain of court martial to go over mach 2.5. If they did, the engines melted.

The threat inflation forces reeled for a while, but they rallied. And after a while, we began to hear, well, actually, you see, we don't realize really how brilliant the Russians are. They designed a fighter for a specific purpose, which was to shoot down American bombers which obviously weren't more than 14 minutes flying time away and this was very cheap, really, because all it has to do was whiz up and shoot down the American bomber and then whiz down again. And, yes, it may have vacuum tube electronics but that's really brilliant because, of course, the Russians figured out long before we did about electromagnetic pulse (EMP), which is a byproduct of nuclear explosions to which modern electronics are very susceptible. How clever they were to have vacuum tubes. And it shows how we underestimate them all the time.

That story, and there are plenty of others, is the classic threat inflation story.

You might say this is all great because although we probably spend too much money on defense, we get a great defense because we're arming to meet something more threatening than the threat actually is. The trouble is the threat we're arming to beat is a totally invented one. So we get a totally unrealistic defense ourselves. The U.S. Navy ignores the Soviet attack submarine fleet because that's bad news for aircraft carriers — but they go on and on about Soviet naval aviation which is rather a puny force. So we have a Navy which is very vulnerable to attack submarines. This is one of the many dangerous byproducts of threat inflation — we get a lousy defense out of it.

Earl C. Ravenal: I tend to find in the range of neoliberal attitudes, especially in matters of national security, more of the old familiar liberal and much less of the neo. To me, neoliberal arguments, just like all liberal arguments that I've heard for two decades, amount to not liking the consequences of present policies rather than repudiating the policies themselves.

Their first fallacy is the fallacy of procurement — that is the belief that the excesses of our whole defense program are somehow a matter of waste, fraud and mismanagement in the Pentagon. For several months now we've been treated to practically a daily soap opera in the newspapers. Journalists have literally been rummaging through parts bins in the military and they've been finding rich fodder for exposes. They finally, I think, have found a defense issue that's worthy of their talents. They've come up with $400 claw hammers and monkey wrenches, and the greatest horror so far, a plastic navigator stool cap from Boeing that cost the Pentagon $916.

The Reagan defense budget request for 1984 was $274 billion, and Congress has not been cutting a great deal out of that. It takes quite a pile of stool caps, claw hammers, step ladders and monkey wrenches, even if they're gold plated or made of titanium, to total up to $274 billion. So I don't think that the matter is one of fraud, waste or mismanagement.

Another fallacy is the notion that the real money in the defense budget somehow lies in a few conspicuous big ticket items. Often cited are the MX missile, B-1 bomber, etc. But those two programs together cost only $6.6 billion and $6.9 billion, respectively, in the administration's 1984 budget request. In short, together they come to less than 5 percent of the total. So that's not the problem.

It might at first seem that the aircraft carrier is one big ticket item that might prove something after all. But as we shall see, the problem with the aircraft carrier, which in a sense is the greatest military horror story of all, is not that it does not work, but in the fact that it does work. The problem is in the normal operation of one of the most basic of this nation's weapons systems, the cornerstone of the Navy, the carrier battle group. It's not in the faulty design of the ship and its complementary aircraft; it's in the economics of modern warfare. With or without a large nuclear aircraft carrier as its centerpiece, an entire carrier battle group, to put that group forward into the eastern Mediterranean or the western Pacific or the Indian Ocean or the north Atlantic, costs over its 30-year lifetime no less than $364 billion, when all the costs are properly distributed and allocated.

Everyone from Robert McNamara to the Catholic bishops would like us to spend more money on conventional forces. Conventional forces are already costing us $212 billion a year, 77 percent of the defense budget. Indeed, an average Army division will cost over $4.5 billion in

1984, and we have 16 of them. A wing of tactical aircraft costs about $1.9 billion; we have the equivalent of 44 of these in the 1984 defense budget or program. The Marine Corps will cost over $18 billion. And the full cost of deploying one aircraft carrier task force is about $12 billion a year and our present strategy requires us to keep four or five of them forward.

Beyond these citations of the costs of our forces it is necessary to make a determination of where in the world we are spending this money. In other words, what are the global geographic missions of these major components of our conventional force structure? In 1984, Europe will cost no less than $115 billion. And Asia will still absorb $45 billion. And the rest of the world (the Pentagon divides the world into these three categories traditionally, including the rapid deployment forces mostly for the Persian Gulf) will take $52 billion.

What is really necessary is a very sharply different approach that responds to the expense of the defense budget by making $100 billion-a-year reductions. That means real reductions that concentrate on the force structure and the doctrine that would lead to strategic stability, and that concentrate on the problem of alliance of the United States from the immense costs and the entailed risks of defending 100 countries around the world—in short, in defending half the world against the other half.

James Fallows: I will toss aside my eloquent set of notes on nuclear policy and, instead, try to make a couple of points that I think Mr. Ravenal may have misstated or may not have stated quite as fairly as he could have.

First, an explanation for the approach many neoliberal writers about defense have taken, including myself. Why have we written about the way a certain weapon works as opposed to "whither NATO?" or "What role for America in the Pacific?" It struck me as an observer of defense debates over the years—not a participant in, but as an observer—that when the debate started where it logically should, with the question of where America should be committed around the world, it never got beyond that. Never. The disagreements were so profound that it's going to be the work of this generation and the next to construct that perfectly logical underpinning for where the forces should be required.

Given that fact of human and political nature, it seemed to me worth trying to short circuit it, at least for a time. If we assume that American foreign policy is going to roll along in basically the same way it has through the post-War generation, what then are the consequences for the force that will be put into being to carry out whatever conceivable policy we're going to have? Whatever the policy, men and women are going to be in the armed forces. They're going to be trained in certain ways; some of those ways will be effective and some will not. Regardless of what our foreign policy is, it's going to have some element in which conventional machines of war do their work. There are going to be fighter planes of some kind, there will be bombers of some kind.

This seemed to be a way to get beyond this absolute logjam of foreign policy discussions. Not that I have no views on foreign policy. But it seemed to me worth getting to the next level, because otherwise that level of analysis was monopolized by John Tower and people of his ilk who had no trouble arguing about foreign policy and just moved right on to the next level.

Whether this approach is merely tinkering on the margins and avoiding the big questions, again I think that is an unfair criticism. For one thing, the sums that Mr. Ravenal gave about the cost of, say, the B-1 and the MX in the 1984 budget, as he knows well, are a fairly dramatic understatement of their eventual cost. In the 1984 budget, neither of these weapons is in full production yet. He very correctly pointed out the whole cost of an aircraft carrier task force over its lifetime. And similarly, if one were to take the cost of these large strategic weapons systems over their lifetimes, one would end up with sizable reductions in the amount of money we're going to devote to the military.

Perhaps it is true that if you were to totally redefine America's interests, especially in Europe, you would end up with a different military force, one dramatically less costly than the one we've had for the last 35 years. If I thought that dramatic step were possible within the next five years, the next 10 years, the next 20 years, then I would join him in saying, well, yes, we can cut off the divisions in this way. As a matter of political reality, I don't think it's possible. But you will, unfortunately, in 1993 have to be using the weapons you decided to build in 1983 when you didn't know at all what the world of 1993 was going to look like.

There is one other element that has a very central role in the defense reform analysis that he doesn't acknowledge at all. That is what one might call the spiritual aspect of these apparently very unspiritual questions. Historians of combat and combat leaders have consistently found that what finally makes a force win or lose is not how many bows and arrows or how many tanks it has, but what its people are like and whether they believe in their cause and trust the people who are leading them. But it's not simply that. It's also the connection between the whole country and the military force that it's deploying around the world. It's for that reason I could not agree more with Senator Hollings when he talked about the importance of a draft as a means for forging this link. This is an old and tired theme for me, but I am impressed by the way he has put it. That spiritual aspect which I think runs through everything people are talking about in this conference, how we can tie our nation's actions to the interests of us all, is at the heart of the entire defense reform debate. It's not about how much a bullet costs or whether or not a tank breaks down, although those things are important. It's about how we as a people carry out this part of our national duty.

A more basic point about the spiritual side: In my view, it is very similar to that about the tax system. I would rather not pay any taxes but I recognize the tax system as an indispensable way of tying everyone's interests to the decisions made in the public's name. The draft seems to me at least as important in the realm of military actions as a way of tying the decisions about where forces will be sent—where Americans will be asked to die—to not having the only people doing the dying be poor people, blacks, and Hispanics. That is what it was during Vietnam, largely because of the student deferment. And it's true of the volunteer force—not right now, because there's 10 percent unemployment, but over the long haul. That's the story of the volunteer army. That seems to me dangerous for democracy and that's why I urge another course.

"Most often, public discussions about defense collapse into the familiar choice between 'more' and 'less' defense, measured solely by money spent and programs begun. For partisans of 'strength' and 'restraint' alike, the unspoken assumption has been that what finally matters in defense is the overall budget figure. To those who favor 'more defense,' a dollar spent on one weapon is about as good as a dollar spent on another. Those who call for 'reordering national priorities' or an end to the arms race are rarely heard supporting any weapon at all. Both sides suffer from the ancient fallacy of measuring input rather than output — judging how hard you try, rather than what you accomplish. Neither goes far toward ensuring that items that would come first, second, third, on any rational list of what the nation needs for defense are the ones we end up having. . . .

"The truly urgent military questions have little to do with how much money we spend. Indeed, more money for defense, without a change in the underlying patterns of spending, will not make us more secure, and may even leave the United States in a more vulnerable position than before."

—James Fallows, *National Defense*

"After leaving the White House, President Dwight Eisenhower observed, 'For eight years (there) I believed . . . that a reduction of American strength in Europe should be initiated as soon as the European economies were restored. I believe the time has now come to start withdrawing some of those troops.'

"That was 20 years ago and nothing has changed. Last year Pentagon officials testified that about half the defense budget — more than $100 billion — is directly or indirectly linked to Europe's protection. While many of the European economies today are even more robust than our own, almost 350,000 American soldiers remain stationed on the continent. That's almost as many as when Eisenhower spoke those words in 1963.

"Of course the U.S. has a vital interest in the security of Western Europe. But the strategic rationale for such a large American force there always has been tenuous. The main function of our troops is to serve as a nuclear 'tripwire.' The theory is that the spilling of American blood on European soil will inevitably mean global nuclear war; knowing that, the Russians will be deterred from such folly.

Is such a large tripwire necessary? Not at all. Only if a future European conflict could be confined to a conventional war would these troops be of much use. But even accepting that dubious assumption, there's the additional question of who should pay for that tripwire. The U.S. now spends far more of its GNP on defense than the NATO allies do to defend, not only their territory, but also their major source of oil: the Persian Gulf... It's time to let Europe be Europe—especially when it comes to paying for its own defense."

> —from "Thirty-five Ways to
> Cut the Defense Budget,"
> *The Washington Monthly,*
> April, 1982

BIBLIOGRAPHY

Articles in **The Washington Monthly**

Easterbrook, Gregg, "The Army's $800,000 Model Airplane," July/August, 1984

Keisling, Phillip, "Our Underworked Air Force," February, 1984

Keisling, Phillip, "Desert One: The Wrong Man and the Wrong Plan," December, 1983

Noah, Timothy, "The Pentagon Press: Prisoners of Respectability," September, 1983

Keisling, Phil, "Soldiers of Good Fortune," May, 1983

Kaplan, Fred, "The Flying Lazarus," February, 1983

Alter, Jonathan, "Misfire: How Pentagon Critics Shot Down Their Own Ace," May, 1982

The Editors, "Thirty-Five Ways to Cut the Defense Budget," April, 1982

Easterbrook, Gregg, "From Sputnik to the Flying Submarine," October, 1981

Easterbrook, Gregg, "All Aboard Air Oblivion," September, 1981

Kaus, Robert M. "Reagan Scorecard," February, 1981

Keller, Bill, "Attack of the Atomic Tidal Wave," May, 1980

Peters, Charles; Greider, William; and Harwood, Richard, "Draft the Rich," April, 1980

Packard, Frank, "The Trident: Our Pre-Sunk Supercarrier," October, 1978

Winslow, John F., "How the Conglomerates Get Free Money from the Navy," November, 1977

Fritchey, Clayton, "The Navy We Need vs. the Navy We've Got," March, 1977

Hopkins, George, "The Better, Cheaper Plane the Pentagon Didn't Want," March, 1977

Rushford, Greg, "How the Condor Was Killed," December, 1976

Rapoport, Daniel, "How F. Edward Herbert Shaved $46 billion from the Defense Budget," November, 1976

Dickson, Paul, "The Robot Airforce," May, 1976

Fairlie, Henry, "National Defense: The Dodos and the Platypuses," February, 1976

La Rocque, Gene, "An Island Paradise for the Admirals," May, 1974

Warnke, Paul, "7,000 toys for the Generals," May, 1974

Schroeder, Pat, "Shooting at Empty Silos," May, 1974

White, William D., "P-38, Where Are You?" December, 1974

Fallows, James, "Crazies by the Tail," September, 1974

Halperin, Morton, "Clever Briefers, Crazy Leaders and Myopic Analysts," September, 1974

Ingram, Timothy H., "Nuclear Hijacking: Now Within the Grasp of Any Bright Lunatic," January, 1973

Hochschild, Adam, "Reserves and Guards: A More Selective Service," January, 1971

Wicklein, John, "The Navy Prepares to Fight World War II," February, 1970

Other Articles

Easterbrook, Gregg, "Divad," *The Atlantic,* October, 1982
Hart, Gary, "What's Wrong with the Military," *The New York Times Magazine,* February 14, 1982
Isaacson, Walter, "Defense Spending: Are Billions Being Wasted?" *Time,* March 7, 1981
Thomson, James, "Why We Are in Vietnam," *The Atlantic,* April, 1968

Books

Cincinnatus, *Self Destruction: The Disintegration and Decay of the U.S. Army During the Vietnam Era*
Cockburn, Andrew, *The Threat: Inside the Soviet Military Machine*
Fallows, James, *National Defense*
Gabriel, Richard and Savage, Paul, *Crisis in Command*
Halberstam, David, *The Best and the Brightest*
Kaplan, Fred, *The Wizards of Armageddon*
Snepp, Frank, *Decent Interval*
The Project on Military Procurement, *More Bucks, Less Bang: How the Pentagon Buys Ineffective Weapons*

Entitlements

THE PANELISTS:

Taylor Branch (moderator) is a contributing editor of *The Washington Monthly* and author of a forthcoming biography of Martin Luther King.
James Fallows is the Washington Editor of *The Atlantic.*
James Capra is a senior economist at Lehmann Brothers Kuhn Loeb and was the Congressional Budget Office's chief of budget projections from 1975 to 1980.
Peter Ferrara served in the Office of Policy Development for Ronald Reagan and is the author of *Social Security: Averting the Crisis.*
Daniel Yankelovich is head of the research firm Yankelovich, Skelly and White and the author of *New Rules.*

Ken Auletta is a writer for *The New
Yorker* and author of *The
Underclass.*

T aylor Branch (Moderator): I think it's rather odd
that we would be sitting here, wringing our hands over entitlement programs. Until 10 or 15 years ago, a conference on
this subject would be almost inconceivable, given the fact
that most of the entitlements we're talking about are the
central part of the legacies of Franklin Roosevelt and Lyndon
Johnson. They lifted a large number of people out of poverty, and have been widely regarded—again, by this liberal
consensus in Americans politics that has operated more or
less on-and-off since Roosevelt—as some of America's
noblest achievements. But there's another strain of thought
now, of course—that all this is heading us to bankruptcy.

Without appearing to take sides, I tend to group entitlements as a whole and call them, for the purposes of this
panel, a beautiful monster. Entitlements have this wonderful history, but now everybody has a sense of foreboding
about it, whether they're liberal or conservative.

One idea I want to introduce, though, by way of a brief
story, is the notion that we're not talking here simply
about welfare and the problems of the poor, although
this is the way the debate has been cast in political terms.
Many of the entitlement programs—unemployment, Social
Security, veterans' benefits, Medicare, Medicaid—do not go
to the poor at all. My story has to do with the birth of my
first child, my daughter, three years ago. Due to overween-
ing honesty, when my wife's employer asked if she would
return after the birth of the child, she said she didn't know.
The net result of that was that our childbirth was not
covered by the employer's health insurance. If she'd lied

and said, "Yes, I do," it would have been covered.

When we went to George Washington University Hospital with her in labor, we were not covered by any insurance whatsoever. I went down to register; she was upstairs. There was a tremendous scurry in the admissions office because the clerks there literally did not know what to do. They called me a "self-pay" and hadn't heard of a self-pay before. What happened after a half-hour of me screaming and everything was that they went upstairs and got an officer of George Washington University Hospital to come down. This lady didn't really know what to do, either, but after a long time she said that the best thing was that I should go get a cashier's check for $2,500 to put up front. Which I did. This was no time to argue. This was not covered in our childbirth class.

I did this, and then I realized that this was a whole new game of "self-pay." After the birth a nurse comes running down the hall with this big tray of goodies. They're all wrapped up and there are plastic bottles and nursers and little diapers and bibs and everything, and she came running in and said, "Here, this is for you." Whereupon I said, "How much does it cost?" I can't tell you how stunned the nurse looked. She went away and brought back the price to me. They were astronomical: $14 for a little plastic bottle. I said I didn't want it and the nurse left.

Within thirty seconds every nurse on the floor knew of me, and I was a marked man. But the reaction of the nurses wasn't nearly as significant to me as the reaction of the other father in the semi-private room, who looked upon me with a look—leper is not quite it—of pity. In his eyes, what I saw him saying to himself was, "I love my wife, I'm an American, I have an insurance policy." What that meant to him was that he was entitled, by being a full-fledged member of American society—which I clearly was not—to medical care more or less on the stolen credit card plan, which is you've got a stolen credit card so don't ask what it costs. And, of course, he never did. So every time the nurse would come in and I would have to ask how much something cost, I would always try to do so out of his eyesight, because he gave me the most withering look.

There's a sequel to the story. Three months ago we had our second child. This time we were shrewd enough so that my wife said she was coming back to work, even though she knew she wasn't. So we were covered. But having questioned the cost when I didn't have any insurance, I felt honor bound to question the cost when I did. So we went in and were processed into the hospital grandly and efficiently and treated like first class guests at a hotel. But when the nurse came in with the same package of everything, I said, "How much does it cost?" The nurse went out, found out that we were covered by insurance, and literally refused to answer the question. "You're insured; it doesn't matter anyway," they said. So I gave up asking.

All this is by way of saying that entitlements are not just the troublesome demands of the poor. Entitlement is also a middle-class phenomenon. Veterans, for example, feel that they are entitled to medical care for their lifetime regardless of whether they're getting care for a war-related wound. Many of us feel entitled to a whole range of things. So we need to make distinctions as to what we're talking about. And whether we're talking about entitlements for the poor or Social Security, we have a sense that we're in trouble, that there's a political problem here that neither the right nor the left in the American dialogue is really saying anything about. Politicians are scared. Basically it's a fear of society being eaten by its larger parts, interest groups driving these things bankrupt.

James Fallows: My role here is to describe the details of the problems that we're grappling with so that other people can give you the answers. I'm glad I have that assignment as opposed to theirs.

There are two large facts about the entitlements situation that predicate the way you look at some of the details. The first large fact is that entitlements now represent almost half of all the money the federal government spends—to be more precise, about 48.5 percent of this year's budget. As a matter of rounding out the rest of the things the federal government does, about 29 percent goes for defense, 12 percent for interest on the debt, and the remaining 10.5 percent for everything else the government does. Now, the significant thing about this is that it represents a dramatic change even from our recent history. As recently as 1970, entitlements were less than one-third of the budget instead of half. In 1955 they were about one fifth of the budget, and in 1941 they were about one-ninth the federal budget. This is by far the fastest growing part of federal obligations. To put it another way, entitlement payments now represent about one dollar out of every nine in the entire gross national product of the United States, whereas in 1965 they were only one dollar out of twenty. So it's a large share, not only of the federal budget, but of our national wealth.

The second significant fact about entitlements is that very few of them are directed at people specifically because they are poor. Most of them are given to people for other reasons, mainly that they have retired or have reached a certain age and are considered to be eligible for payments. Of this half of the budget devoted to entitlements, five-sixths is for "non-means tested entitlements," a famous phrase you'll hear many times today. Roughly one-sixth goes for "means tested entitlements" such as food stamps or Aid to Families with Dependent Children—programs for which you have to demonstrate some kind of financial need to qualify.

It is true that some of the non-means tested entitlements help poor people, too. And it can be argued persuasively that because of two non-means tested entitlements — Social Security and Medicare — the elderly who used to be impoverished as a class no longer are so. So it's misleading to claim that this five-sixths versus one-sixth division tells you how much goes to people who are really poor. Nonetheless, I think that this second fact is important to bear in mind as a way of contrasting the normal public rhetoric, which equates entitlements with welfare. It's also a way of understanding the political problem of controlling entitlements. When the major beneficiaries are everybody, not just those unpopular poor people, it is much harder to rein the payments in.

The largest of the non-means tested programs is Social Security, which will cost, this year, something in the neighborhood of $180 billion. This represents about 20 percent of the entire federal budget. The next largest of the categorical programs is Medicare, started in 1965. It is smaller than Social Security by a factor of about three but is growing much faster. When the program was established in 1965, congressional budget analysts said, well, we expect a cost of about $9 billion by 1990. In fact, it reached that in 1972, and it's now about $50 billion. Next on the list of these categorical programs are things like civil service retirement, military retirement, and others.

Of the entitlements that are means tested, Medicaid is the largest. It now costs about $18 billion. To keep that in perspective, that's about one-tenth as large as Social Security. Next down is food stamps at about $10 billion. To keep that in perspective, it's about one-half as large as civil service retirement. Then there's AFDC, which is now about $8 billion.

These programs have grown so quickly for several reasons. One is that the population is older, which matters because so many of these benefits are retirement benefits. In 1950 about one American out of 43 drew benefits from Social Security; right now it's about one in seven. People are living longer, retiring earlier, spending more of their lives drawing benefits. A second factor is the indexing pathology of federal programs. Over the last decade, people who are on indexed benefits came out ahead in the inflationary spiral. The third reason is the chain letter philosophy of Social Security. This has been a system premised on the promise that everyone will get back more than he put in. That can be sustained for a while, as long as the population is growing rapidly and the national wealth is expanding as it did during the 1960s. But at a certain point there's nobody else you can send the chain letter to. That is the point we're at with Social Security, and many of these others.

I think there are three painful choices that we have to face in figuring out a neoliberal answer, or any answer, to these problems. The first is figuring out, simultaneously, how to make these programs stop costing so much or stop growing so quickly while giving more money to certain people who now qualify under the program. What I have in mind here is that even though Social Security has been expanding so rapidly, half of all the single women in this country over the age of 65 live on an entire annual income, including Social Security, of less than $5,000. That's half of all the nation's single, retired women. They need more money. If they are to have more money, and if the programs are going to be contained, I think there has to be a breaking of the historical promise of Social Security, which is that everybody would receive benefits equally. That's my first painful choice.

The second painful choice is what to do about medical costs, which are the engines of the fastest growth within the entitlement programs as a whole. You see that in the way Medicare is expected to cost more than Social Security within the next two decades or so. This brings us into the realm of such prescriptions as drafting the doctors. I always declare a hands-off policy here because my father is a doctor, a man I admire greatly, and so this is one area of the neoliberal philosophy from which I take a distance.

The third choice, and I think the most difficult one for liberals of any kind even to talk about, is to consider, for that part of the American population that is poor and depends for its survival on government largesse, how this support can be provided without creating a culture that impedes the movement of that populace out of their circumstances. That is the third choice and I think the liberals' dirty little secret is figuring out how to deal with that.

James Capra: I think it's useful to talk about the recent changes in Social Security for two reasons. First, it's a subject that's interesting in and of itself. Second, many think that the Social Security problem has now been solved.

The problems that the legislation was responding to were twofold: near-term insolvency—there would soon have been no trust fund money to write checks—and long-term bankruptcy. There is no way taxes could come close to covering the benefits that were scheduled in the long run. For the short term a number of changes were made. These changes appear to have provided sufficient assets for the system to make its way through the 1980s and actually the 1990s. Tax-increase accelerations, limited taxation of benefits, cost-of-living adjustment delays, and a goodly amount of bookkeeping adjustments — general fund transfers, really—appear to have done the trick. If we have a recession between now and 1988, then there well could be problems. But as things stand now under the commonly used assumptions, the legislation has solved the near-term insolvency problem.

The second problem still facing us is the long-term bankruptcy of the system. Under Social Security, as it was prior to the new legislation, the present value return for an employer/employee contribution — sort of an actuarial return with interest and inflation and everything taken into account — was well above the contributions themselves. Everybody was getting a windfall out of Social Security and everybody was scheduled to get a windfall forever. This obviously couldn't continue. There were some esoteric theories that suggested that it could, but those theories didn't correspond to the real world where birth rates fluctuate up and down, productivity rates fluctuate up and down, etc. Consequently, the system was scheduled to go bankrupt. The changes that were made — various types of changes such as taxing benefits and raising the retirement age — all affect the returns to taxpayers or returns to future beneficiaries.

What ended up happening for the long run is that the ratio of the present value of benefits to the present value of taxes is scheduled to dip below one. In other words, people will get less, on a present value basis, than they put in, beginning just after the year 2000. This is for the average wage earner.

The implication I draw from this is that support for the system under the legislation as it's currently being enacted is going to erode as people start to realize they're getting out a lot less than they put in. You already hear people saying, or you've already heard people say over the last 10 or 15 years, "Why should I participate in Social Security, because I get out less than I put in?" That was what they were saying when they in fact were getting out a lot *more* than they were putting in. Now people will actually get less than they put in, and, consequently, my prediction is that Social Security will have to be a part of a major restructuring of the federal budget over the next 10 years or so.

Peter Ferrara: Social Security remains plagued by financing problems. The recent bail out didn't solve it. And over the long term, the projections showing the actuarial balance of Social Security are based on quite unrealistic assumptions. The most reasonable projections show that in order to pay the benefits that are being promised to those entering the work force today, the payroll tax rates will have to be raised to 25 or 30 percent of taxable income, compared to 13 percent today. A former chief actuary of the Social Security Administration, Hayeworth Robertson, projects that those payroll tax rates will have to climb to 40 percent compared to 15 percent today. And I just want to say that one thing that liberals need to come to recognize more is that believing the Social Security Administration about the Social Security program and its projections is the same thing as believing the Defense Department at face value about the M-1 tank.

This collapse of the return paid by Social Security is a natural consequence of its method of operation. The system operates on a pay-as-you-go basis. The money paid into the system is immediately paid out to current beneficiaries. There's no savings made. One thing that means is that when the program started up, those workers who were already in the work force only had to pay taxes for their remaining working years, yet they received full benefits when they retired. The taxes in the initial years of the program were also quite low. The maximum Social Security tax, including the employer share, was $189 as late as 1958, and $348 as late as 1965. Over time, as workers began to be paying higher taxes for more of their working career, their return from the system (when they retired) naturally began to fall. Those retirees who currently retire are still getting a good deal from the system. But young workers who are entering the work force today will pay taxes of several thousand dollars a year for their entire working careers. The maximum annual tax today is $4,784; by the end of the decade the Social Security Administration projects it will be close to $8,000. So even if all the promised benefits to today's young workers are somehow paid, the program will still be a miserable deal. If they were allowed to take that Social Security tax money and put it in an IRA, those entering the work force today could receive several times the benefits that they could get under the Social Security system.

Another problem with the program is the payroll tax, which has not been particularly focused on as an independent problem. The payroll tax is basically a tax on the act of employment. To the extent the tax is borne by the employer, it discourages him from offering a job; to the extent it is borne by the employee, it discourages him from taking a job. The result of the payroll tax is that the higher it's raised, the more it crushes employment and crushes employment opportunities. Today, for at least half of all workers covered by Social Security, the combined payroll tax is more than they pay in federal income tax. For a society concerned about employment opportunities, this huge tax burden on the act of employment is absolutely crazy.

Daniel Yankelovich: On the matter of entitlements, I really want to make just a single point. From the thirties to the seventies liberalism exercised great political influence because it appealed to the center. And I believe that one of the main reasons, and perhaps the principal reason, that liberalism is in political trouble with the center today revolves around the doctrine of entitlements that took shape in the 1960s.

Let me start with a few of the assumptions that underlie the doctrine. All Americans should be entitled, as a matter of legal as well as moral right, to have their basic needs met. Basic needs include food, shelter, jobs, medical care, education, and justice. If certain groups of people demand something, that is evidence that they need it. The society is obligated to meet these needs. The recipient incurs no obligation. He or she is simply receiving what he or she is entitled to as a matter of moral and legal right. The country is rich enough to guarantee these rights through government-sponsored entitlement programs without really hurting those with means. Benefits can be distributed without the cost being felt so that the redistribution is not really a zero sum game since there's enough wealth to go around. And in the event of conflict between rights based on needs versus rights based on some other principle of deserving, need-based entitlements are to have priority.

These are just a few, not all, of the assumptions, but that's probably the heart of the doctrine. The heart of the doctrine is that the theory of need-based rights, need-based entitlements, is in contrast to the popular view that fairness is getting what you deserve and getting what you deserve means you have to do something. If you've worked hard, you deserve a raise. If you've been loyal, you deserve loyalty in return. If you're smart, you may deserve a chance at an education. If you've observed all the rules, you deserve a certain respect and recognition.

In the 1960s the electorate embraced both doctrines until contradictions and conflicts began to appear between them. To me the prototypical conflict of the sixties was if you could visualize two neighbors with the same income living next door to each other. Both of them have children who want to go to college. One has scrimped and scraped and saved and he doesn't get the grant-in-aid because he doesn't "need" it; his neighbor who has been profligate gets it.

It's that kind of conflict that has confused the electorate and finally driven them to begin to oppose, not necessarily in conceptual terms but instinctively and increasingly, this notion of need-based entitlements. And I would put the political issue as sharply as possible, which is to say that today — and for the last five or six years — in every instance where the two doctrines conflict, the public, in contrast to the liberal position, will favor the doctrine of fairness based on deserving rather than the doctrine of fairness based on need.

Ken Auletta: You can tell the difference between a liberal, a conservative, and a neoliberal by talking about welfare. The liberal will tend to say that all the people on welfare are victims of forces beyond their control, be it the economy or racism. The conservative will tend to say that they're all a bunch of villains, or most of them are. What a neoliberal should say is that some are villains and some are victims.

First, I should start by saying that entitlements, including the welfare entitlement, have performed some very valuable functions. Many people that I observed over the course of two and a half years of doing my book who had received welfare — I daresay probably most — had been helped by it to escape poverty. In fact, of the 30-odd million Americans classified as poor, studies at the University of Michigan — which is the only place that has done what they call longitudinal surveys of people who have been poor over a number of years — show that two-thirds of people who are poor in America have mobility. The American dream, though imprecisely, tends to work. They climb out of their poverty. The children are not like the parents in that respect.

However, there's one-third that remains, a group of

Americans who tend to be mired in poverty inter-generationally. This is the group that I call the "underclass." The underclass is not just a group of Americans who are poor. In fact, many members of the underclass are in fact people who make a very extraordinary living in the under-ground economy and the criminal economy, going at a career in crime the way some of us go at a career in writing. The bad news about this underclass, something that liberals tend to overlook and not talk about, is welfare dependency. In 1960 three million families were on welfare. By 1980, over 10 million American families were on welfare. More tellingly, 40 percent of those people on welfare had been on welfare three or more years. If you go to West Virginia, where I spent some time, you'll find that the AFL–CIO ran a supportive work program and the biggest single recruitment problem they had was that 25 percent of the mothers—these were all white mothers, by the way—25 percent of them were afraid to leave their home for the security of a guaranteed job, even though that guaranteed job paid more than welfare. Welfare for them had become a habit. It's a fairly significant number of people, a number that may actually grow as we see the growing incidence of teenage pregnancy, with young girls mothering young kids for whom welfare becomes a way of life.

Welfare clearly has to have some consequence. How much of a consequence has not been measured, but it has to have some consequence in terms of the social revolution that is taking place in our society. Once again, liberals tend not to talk about that; in fact, most conservatives tend not to talk about it. I certainly haven't heard Ronald Reagan talk about it. And that is what is happening to the family.

In 1940, when we had Jim Crow laws and racism was much worse in the society and social spending was much less, 15 percent of all black children in this country were born out of wedlock. By 1979, 55 percent were born out of wedlock. Something must explain that rise in family break-up at a time when the economy had actually been performing better than it had been in 1940, when racism was less and when government spending was more generous. Something happened out there.

One hypothesis for what happened is that welfare somehow contributed to the break-up of the family. Many liberals would agree with that; in almost half the states there's a requirement that to receive welfare, the man cannot be present or the spouse not be present if they're able-bodied. Otherwise you cannot receive welfare. It is presumed that many men have been chased out of the house, and there is no question in my mind that there's some truth to this. But there's also some truth to some other sides of that equation, including the fact that the welfare system creates a feeling on the part of many recipients of helplessness, that I'm entitled, that I'm going to be taken care of—and me, the male, I'm not responsible, government is. There were too many people that I interviewed who, in their own words, said just that for me not to believe there's some truth to it, even though it tends to fly in the face of things we would rather believe.

When we talk about poverty, we tend to fall into the trap of talking about what I call "yes-or-no politics." That is to say, the poor were either victims or villains, society or the individual was to blame, there was either no progress or there was lots of progress. It seems to me that when you look at social welfare programs in this country, a much more intelligent position to take is to say that, in fact, both positions are true.

Yes, there's clear racism in the society and it's not always obvious racism. One of the things that stunned me in living with a group of Americans whom I classified as belonging to the underclass was the people who said they had never experienced racism themselves. Many of these people had never left the ghetto, had never left their own little community, had very little dealings with the white world. Yet they felt inferior. This psychological dimension of racism seems to me worth much more exploration by many in the progressive community. Yet while there is racism in our society, real and imagined, it's not the sole explanation, for instance, for what has happened to· the black and Puerto Rican family.

Yes, the Great Society helped some people, many people. You can point to Social Security cutting in half the poverty among senior citizens. But like Vietnam, there is no total victory when you're talking about the underclass or dealing with poverty in America. Traditional conservatives have a measure of truth on their side when they talk about the fact that it takes time to solve some problems, that it may take some decentralized approaches, that it takes an acceptance of responsibility on the part of the individual receiving the service to help climb out of their poverty. Yet traditional liberals have truth on their side when they talk about how it also takes a government's helping hand, because many of these people are not "economic" for the business person making an investment. It also takes the individual attention that liberals have talked about.

I don't mean this as a cop-out, but it's really important before one can talk about solutions to be sure we understand the nature of the problem and the causes of it. If you go and look at the causes of teenage pregnancy, you'll find them much more complex than just the simple suggestion that they're having babies to get welfare. Many of the young women I spent a fair amount of time with talked about some of the following reasons. They wanted something to love. They wanted to escape their mothers, or the domination of the bad family situation, including some violence in the home. They wanted to attract the boyfriend.

They didn't know about birth control, or they didn't know how it worked. They thought that the man had birth control. So the answer to the problem of what do you do about teenage pregnancy is not a single answer, it seems to me. It's a multiple answer that talks about sex education, which conservatives don't want to talk about, but that talks about values as well, which liberals tend not to want to talk about. Many of these young girls I encountered were ashamed. In fact, one of the things that is actually depressing is that the level of shame is probably going down as it becomes more acceptable to have a child, which again gets back to a value question. I think the schools have some role here. You might think about, in some cases, forcing the family to take some more responsibility, and in some cases you wouldn't want the family to take responsibility because you really want to get that kid away from the family she's in.

Question: Economists such as Walter Williams and Thomas Sowell have looked at the other side of the welfare state, all the restrictions—licensing laws, the density zoning requirements, minimum wage laws—that exclude people from the marketplace and keep them from learning a trade. I wonder if part of the neoliberal approach to poverty might be to take this into account, namely, that people are institutionally barred from the job market and once they are barred from it, they are then manipulated and made dependent by the welfare system.

James Fallows: I've spent much of the last year traipsing around the country in search of immigrants and the people they compete with, and one thing is clear that does support something of the conservative view: when freed from direct impediments to their advancement, these people get ahead and do so very quickly. And you see a difference between legal and illegal immigrants. The illegal ones can't typically get a bank loan, they can't buy a house, they can't get into the normal economy, so they don't rise as quickly. The legal immigrants are usually able to zip ahead.

On the specific point of the minimum wage as a tool to open up opportunities, my mind has been changed about that by going out and seeing people. I used to think there was something to be said for the idea that the minimum wage was a big impediment. When you see how many people in this country earn $3.35 because that's the minimum wage, and who would be earning $2 an hour if it weren't for that, and then you consider how little money $3.35 an hour is for people to live on, I don't have much sympathy for reducing that because you would instantly lower the standard of living for a lot of people who are working very hard. So that particular barrier doesn't seem very persuasive to me any more.

Question: Who on the panel favors a negative income tax or a guaranteed national income?

Ken Auletta: I don't think a guaranteed national income is the answer. There are advantages to such a system. It might reduce bureaucracy. It might remove the stigma of welfare, which is very real. It might lessen pressures on the family. But it seems to me the **disadvantages** of a guaranteed national income — which is a proposal that's supported, by the way, by some traditional conservatives as well as traditional liberals and some neoliberals — outweigh the advantages. First and foremost, such a program would reinforce, or potentially reinforce, dependency which is, in fact, one of the major problems with welfare. I don't think you lift that sense of what columnist William Raspberry calls "victimism" by giving everyone a guarantee.

If you want to do something about the underclass, if you accept the assumption that I accept—that this issue in effect is the liberals' domestic nuclear bomb—then you've got to go with some approaches that are at the margins, which assume that government provides help but also assume that the individual has to bring certain attitudes and values to that helping hand that they receive from government.

Taylor Branch: I favored the family assistance plan which came very, very near to getting passed in the early 1970s. This was the Pat Moynihan proposal, which is somewhat like a guaranteed annual income and is not necessarily unfeasible. It was torpedoed by a rather odd combination of the radical left, the social services bureaucracy, and the radical right. It was a very odd phenomenon at an odd point in time.

My basic answer to Ken Auletta is that I don't see that the family assistance plan or something similar has any more stigma or any more "culture of dependency" built in than the current system. So I think it's a good thing to try.

James Fallows: I'll throw in a pitch for something like a negative income tax, because to me the point of that is you stop having 98,000 different reasons that people get money from the government. If they're over 65 and once worked for the railroad, if they're under 18 and have a kid—we should say, instead, we'll give money to people who need it and not to people who don't need it. That seems to me the general neoliberal direction for entitlements. You can't afford to give money to everybody, so you give it to the people who need it.

Taylor Branch: One of the weird things with the

family assistance plan that contributed to its defeat was that there were some very sophisticated people who said they voted against it precisely because they were afraid it would bring into sharp relief the amount of money that goes to people who don't need it as opposed to people who do need it. The people who get entitlements are very sophisticated politically, and we, the people who are trying to figure out what to do about it, are not sophisticated politically.

BIBLIOGRAPHY

Articles in The Washington Monthly

Olson, Mancur, "What We Lose When the Rich Go on the Dole," January, 1984

Keisling, Phil, "Protection from Catastrophe: The Medicare Reform We Really Need," November, 1983

Longman, Phillip, "Taking America to the Cleaners," November, 1982

Keisling, Phil, "Old Soldiers Never Die," March, 1982

Boyd, Marjorie, "Pensions: The Five Trillion Dollar Scandal," February, 1978

Lemann, Nicholas, "Antisocial Security," January, 1978

Fialka, John J., "Battle of the Barons," May, 1976

Marx, Lenny, "Confessions of an Unemployment Cheat," May, 1976

Starr, Paul, "The $12 Billion Misunderstanding: Veterans and the VA," November, 1973

Branch, Taylor, "Patrick Moynihan's Ship of Fools," January, 1973

Friedman, Milton, "Social Security: The Poor Man's Welfare Payment to the Middle Class," May, 1972

Other Articles

Capra, James and Skaperdas, Peter, "Social Security: An Analysis of Its Problems," *Federal Reserve Bank of New York Quarterly Review,* Autumn, 1982

Fallows, James, "Entitlements," *The Atlantic,* November, 1982

Peterson, Peter, "Social Security: The Coming Crash," and "The Salvation of Social Security," *The New York Review of Books,* December 2 and 16, 1982

Books

Auletta, Ken, *The Underclass*

Crystal, Stephen, *America's Old Age Crisis*

Ferrara, Peter, *Social Security: Averting the Crisis*

Kutza, Elizabeth Ann, *The Benefits of Old Age: Social Welfare Policy for the Elderly*

Moynihan, Daniel Patrick, *The Politics of a Guaranteed Annual Income*

Democratic Accountability

THE PANELISTS:

Walter Isaacson (moderator) is an editor of *Time*.

Robert M. Kaus is politics editor of *Harper's*.

Charles Peters is the editor of *The Washington Monthly.*

Peter Shapiro is the county executive of Essex County, New Jersey.

Walter Shapiro is an associate editor of *Newsweek*.

Curtis Gans is director of The Committee for the Study of the American Electorate.

Walter Isaacson (Moderator): What we're really talking about here today, to put it bluntly, is politics, a wonderful and glorious and someday, I hope, no longer a dirty word. It's a word for what we mean when we say that our government should be accountable to the people, when we say that our campaigns should be accountable to the people, and when we say that we're trying to have a government for and by the people.

The two major things we're going to touch on today are how we choose our leaders through the political process, through open and fair elections that reflect the will of the people; and secondly, how do we get government to reflect the mandate that the electorate gives its leaders, how do we get government to be accountable to the will of the people?

Robert M. Kaus: At the risk of establishing myself as the most irresponsible practitioner of the politics of responsibility, I am going to talk about the Constitution. The Constitution is one of the great unquestioned assumptions of liberalism. We're so terrified that somebody is going to want to abolish the first amendment, as people have been known to propose from time to time, that we tend to say, "Let's just not talk about the Constitution." It's sacrosanct, it's almost a religious document. We're scared of even bringing up any possible flaws in it because we're worried that Jesse Helms might take control. That's a completely pragmatic and accurate attitude if you think the constitution is working. I just have my doubts that the structure the founding fathers set up is really working to produce a government that can be effectively controlled by the people.

The founding fathers were obsessed with preventing the tyranny of the majority. They solved that problem in the Constitution by making it very difficult for the government, through various checks and balances, to do anything. We divided the legislature from the executive branch. We divided the legislature within itself into two houses that both had to agree. We gave their members differing terms; we made those terms different from the term of the president. All of this was designed, as Madison said, to make sure that any political conflagration or faction didn't sweep through the whole house, to make it very hard for any massive outpouring of popular will to effect dramatic change.

This was tolerable until we discovered during the Depression that our government really had a lot more governing to do than it did in 1789. And then what did we do? As we realized that the three branches the founding fathers set up couldn't handle the load of all the rules and regulations that had to be written, we created a fourth branch of government—the administrative state. We staffed it with experts and we told them to go write rules and regulations that had the effect of law. Congress would give them some vague injunction like "protect the public health and safety where appropriate." But then we didn't really believe our own rhetoric about how these were impartial experts, and since Congress didn't really have time to oversee them, we subjected them to the supervision of the least democratic of all our branches, the courts.

The result is a system by which unelected bureaucrats decide on regulations, they're appealed by unelected lawyers, and then finally decided on by unelected judges. For example, I may support air bags, but the people who elected Reagan clearly knew he was going to get rid of the air bag rule. Yet a court came in and second guessed him. I think that's wrong. I don't think that's democracy. I don't like Reagan's decision, but in a democracy the leaders we elect have to put their program into effect, whether it's right or wrong, and then we can see the results. We can see the people being killed on the highway—and then we can get Reagan out of there.

There are various gradations of possible reforms aimed at uniting the two branches of government—legislative and executive—with bonds of political accountability. Right now what happens often is the president proposes something; the Congress may be in control of the other party and doesn't pass it. The president then blames the Congress, the Congress blames the president, the public doesn't really know who to blame, and responsibility sort of falls through the cracks. Usually what happens is we throw out the president and keep our incumbent congressmen.

To give the president more of a whip hand over Congress, you could allow the president to pose a referendum once or twice a term on a specific issue. He could write the law, and this would be a club he could hold over the Congress, saying, "Look, if you don't go along with this I'm going to go over your heads to the people." Governor Reubin Askew used this power very effectively in Florida.

Another power we might give the president is the power to appoint the chairmen of Congressional committees and to allocate committee assignments. This prospect is, of course, terrifying to the powers in the Senate and Congress who currently enjoy their power precisely because they have those prerogatives. But it would certainly be effective for precisely that reason, giving the president control over his troops in Congress. It would even help in working with the other party; if you were a Democratic president, even if Republicans controlled the Senate you could appoint Chuck Percy chairman of the Foreign Relations Committee instead of Jesse Helms. You'd at least have a Congress you could work with better than is often now the case.

The most radical but also the most effective of these reforms is a proposal made by former Representative Jonathan Bingham—and then later disavowed by him—to require the president to run on an unsplittable ticket with the members of his party who are running for Congress. This would make the members of Congress and the president very concerned about working together because, if they screwed up, they would both hang together as opposed to hanging separately.

Charles Peters: When I was in the West Virginia legislature, I wrote the West Virginia civil service law. I wrote it for a state that had a completely patronage system. Seeing a total patronage system made me well aware that this was not a good thing.

Then, because I worked for Jack Kennedy in West Virginia in 1960, I was offered a job in Washington. I came here and saw the complete opposite system, where the town was 99 percent civil service. I saw that while there was something wrong with the all-patronage system that we had had in West Virginia, there sure as hell was something wrong with the all civil service system we had here.

Let me tell you about that experience of being appointed to the federal government. I was one of just 2,000 to 2,500 appointments that Kennedy had available to him at that time, and it's no more today. That's less than one-tenth of one percent of the federal work force. I would never have been appointed to that job, or even had a chance for that job, except for a total accident of history. The West Virginia primary happened to be important enough to the Kennedys and since I was practically the only troop there for a while, they had to get to know me. And even though I could be a difficult person, naturally a certain gratitude develops to your only troop on the scene. So they said, "Do something with him," and they put me in the Peace Corps.

My point is that for a career in politics there is so little reward open today, so little to aim for. I'm not talking about reward in terms of getting a nice salary or something like that. I mean the reward in the sense of the chance to carry out the programs you had worked for in the election, the programs you believe in. That's the kind of reward I mean, the kind of reward good people in politics want.

At Yale they now have a course in politics that's just about the business of getting people to the polls and that kind of stuff. It's not about the art of turning elections into programs. Yet *that's* what politics is. These poor fools have gotten so confused by the civil service idea that they think the only thing you're talking about when you say "politics" is somebody working at the polls. Well, that's wrong, it's silly, and it's a terrible thing that's happened in this country. What politics should be is a whole life committed to connecting your programs, your philosophy, your ideas with the life of politics.

In West Virginia I had a little plan that's kind of like what I propose now. I had about 40 percent of the state put under the civil service. Well, now it's 95 percent there. In state after state you now have this same situation of almost no opportunity. And what do we have as a result? We have the decline of the political parties. And what do we have rising instead of the political parties? The special interest groups.

What I would do is have a system that is roughly 50 percent civil service. There is advantage to these people: they give you continuity, they have an institutional memory, and they are guards against the occasional abuses to which all politicians are sometimes subject. On the other hand, with the half that has been in politics, you get a different kind of personality. The ordinary person that is drawn to civil service is attracted to job security. That means he is likely to lack certain risk-taking qualities, that he is likely to lack imagination and daring. You get another kind of person when he is willing to risk being thrown out in three or four years. And that's what I'd have. I'd have short-term appointments, maybe 2½ to 5 years.

It's important to emphasize also that if you have such a system of politics, you have to make the decision on the person who just worked for you. My cousin Suzie might have killed herself at the polls, but if she can only type 20 words a minute and she wants a job as a typist, I can't give it to her. I don't want a system of politics where we give Suzie that job if she can only type 20 words a minute. She has to be qualified to do that job. But if she's qualified, and if she worked hard in our campaign and wants to be part of putting our program into effect, I want her over somebody who doesn't give a damn about our program.

There will be a good result of such a system on the civil service, in the kind of people you get to come into politics, on the number of people pursuing careers in politics, and on the revitalization of the political parties. The last good effect is that it sends people back into the country who have had experience in government, who know what the problems are in government, who can vote intelligently. Let's say the nation hears something like, oh, there's this colossal budget deficit, what the hell do we do about that? Well, people who have been in government and have some idea where the fat is in government will be able to pressure their Congressmen from the standpoint of knowing what really goes on in Washington. Just think what you'd have if you had 50 percent of the government turning over every two or three years, of new people coming in and new people going back home. You would have a citizenry that was informed, that was sophisticated about this government, and would be able to bring to bear on their representatives an informed pressure for good.

Peter Shapiro: I'm the county executive of Essex County, New Jersey. Its largest city is Newark, and Essex County is the largest local government in New Jersey. It has about 7,000 employees, and that's after we pruned back about 20 percent of the work force in the last 5 years. I negotiate with about 35 unions that represent those 7,000 employees, which adds a whole different coloration to the way government has to be managed.

When I was first elected I often worked very late at night, trying to figure out how things worked. I'd be up in my office and occasionally there would be other employees working as part of the maintenance crews who would stumble down the halls. One night I ran into a guy and I said to him, "What kind of employee are you?" And he said, "I'm a B employee." I said, "What do you mean, a B employee?" And he said, "Well, I be here before you were here and I be here while you're here and I be here after you're here." It sort of summarized to me how great the problem is of really trying to accomplish change in government.

Our system in Essex County is a very strong civil service system, but it is one where creative and clever minds sitting in positions of power have always been able to figure out how to effectively subvert it. It's really a fairly easy thing to do, and I'll describe to you briefly how it's done.

Number one, you try to maximize the number of unclassified positions not technically covered by the civil service. Out of 7,000 employees, maybe 100 are unclassified, that is, technically non-civil service. But there is another category of employees called "permanent noncompetitives" who fill titles like laborer, hospital attendant, clerk/typist. In effect, you can take whomever you want off the street, plug them into one of those slots, and after 90 days they become permanent. Then there are seasonal and temporary employees who work for less than a full year. They, by and large, are also not covered by the civil service system. Then there are "provisional employees" who you can put into a position where there is not yet an active civil service examination list. One of the typical things that's done is as soon as you've got your people in those provisional titles and the exam finally gets called, you change the title. It's a very common thing. I said about 100 jobs were technically unclassified, but probably 1,500 are under one or another of these titles.

The problems with patronage have been oft discussed. They include the lack of safeguards for employees; the fact that they can be subject to arbitrary actions on the part of the employer; the general tendency to avoid efficiency because of a desire not to prune back your work force; the general desire to make the work force expand over time; and some of the worst abuses of nepotism and favoritism that can go on. New Jersey has some famous history of such abuses, as do many other urban parts of the country. The Jersey City Medical Center, for instance, was built by one of the great patronage leaders of all time, Frank Hague. His successor didn't have quite the same zeal for health care that he did, and put people on the hospital's work force who were actually living in Florida.

So there are problems with patronage to be on guard against. But ultimately the best remedy is not putting everybody under civil service, but when it's abused, to throw the people out of office. The question really gets down to whether, in guaranteeing that abuses will never occur, is it worth it to mediocratize the rest of government?

Walter Shapiro: I ran for Congress 11 years ago. I faced the voters in the second district of Michigan and I finished second in a contested Democratic primary. And in the ensuing 11 years I have discovered that mentioning this is a sure-fire way of having a hush fall over one of those fashionable dinner parties with lawyers, investment bankers, former Carter administration officials, journalists. The reason is that there's a sense among such people that politics is dirty, that politics is something that nice Jewish boys don't get into. To them, politics is writing memos, advising candidates. And I think that says something very bad about the system, about what has become the calling of politics.

Part of the problem is the lack of accountability in Congress to anyone other than special interest groups. A main reason for that, as we all know, is the prodigiously high cost of campaigning. This has been one of the subjects that has occupied good government types for the last

15 years. It was the main reason that Common Cause came into being. But as for making politics more fair or more accessible to people like 25-year-old unemployed graduate students who don't own a car and get around on a bicycle to get to Congress, the reforms of recent years have failed abysmally. If anything, in the last couple of years, as Elizabeth Drew and countless others can testify, the situation has gotten appallingly worse. No one has been able to devise a mechanism for reforming campaign spending that will pass the United States Congress, whose members have more than a passing bit of self-interest in the problem.

We've gotten into a fairly sterile debate. On one hand you have the people who look at Congress and say it doesn't mirror the United States—there aren't enough women, there aren't enough blacks, there aren't enough 25-year-old graduate students. On the other hand you have the purists who say, "Oh my God, they're selling Congressmen like they're selling soap. There are campaign advertisements that don't even talk about substance. Why, if only we could have four- or five- or six-hour League of Women Voters' forums."

We need campaign reform, but not the campaign reform that gives us the Federal Election Commission and some of the procedural awkwardness of the current presidential campaign. We need campaign reform that at least lessens the special interest stranglehold in Congress. Every incumbent now has to worry about raising $500,000 to $1 million for a contested House race, and that means a constant, nonstop round of fundraisers starting about two months after their election.

The solution, I think, is to appeal to the incumbent's self-interest and put a limit on the amount of money you can spend in a Congressional campaign—say, $300,000. This will appeal to incumbents because their big fear is the millionaire who'll come in and spend $1.5 million to beat them. Such a ceiling will allow incumbents not to go into hock to special interest groups, yet is probably low enough to permit a volunteer-based Congressional campaign to succeed. More importantly, since it is not funding the opponents of incumbent Congressmen, it has a fighting chance of passing Congress.

There's one other point I want to add, about patronage. I served in the Carter administration, and I think to a large extent the experience was a small version of what Charlie was talking about. I was in the Labor Department, which then had a work force of about 10,000 people, a discretionary budget of about $20 billion, and a fairly large mandate to put America back to work. It had exactly 70 political appointees. Jimmy Carter even frittered that away since of the 70 he appointed, only 4 had actually worked in his campaign. The analogy I came up with is that of the Spanish conquistadors suddenly finding themselves in Mexico City. The civil servants were all bowing down to us as if we were some sort of diety, yet they were babbling in these strange tongues and following these strange practices. So we immediately took on this total garrison mindset of talking only to ourselves and a few quislings in the civil service. One of the legacies of this sort of adversarial response, I believe, is that public service jobs, which I still think are the best governmental response to high unemployment, has now become one of these discredited political notions that will probably next surface in about the year 2010.

Curtis Gans: In 1980 the cost of all political campaigns in the U.S. was $1.2 billion. In 1982, without the benefit of a presidential campaign, the costs of all campaigns was still over $1 billion. In the last two decades the actual cost, in constant dollars, of political campaigns has tripled; in just the last decade it's doubled.

This has largely been caused by the transfer of campaigns to electronic media and television. The typical campaign, which used to spend a lot of money on other means, now spends between half and two-thirds of its budget on television. That has also led to a diminution of spending on things that involve political participation. I wrote once that we are approaching the silent spring of American politics, in which buttons, bumper stickers, storefronts, and popular involvement are all becoming a thing of the past. What we have is talking cows replacing talking politicians. We have demagogic devices replacing debates. Perhaps more important, we have the political consultant replacing the political party as the point of entry for candidates. It is not a coincidence, I believe, that in the two decades that television has become a central factor in American political life, voter participation in general has been going down.

I'd like to offer an idea that is being practiced presently in France which has merit and a possibility of success here. That idea is simply to require that paid political advertising on television be without production material—no voice overs, no graphs, no anonymous faces, no talking cows, no actors playing parts, no little girls with daisies. Let us allow the candidates, the party chairmen, the interest group leaders to buy whatever time they want to buy, to say whatever they want to say—as long as they do the same.

I think the public deserves a right to see what they're buying, and not through filters. I do not believe that politicians should, or need necessarily be, sold as soap. Secondly, I think there is a responsibility that needs to be put at the doorsteps of candidates, the parties, and the interest groups for the negative campaigning that they want to do. If they want to bad mouth their opponent, let *them* say it—not through an anonymous face or a voice over.

I think this will reduce the power of consultants in American politics and, by virtue of that, indirectly enhance the power of elected officials in parties. It will deal creatively with the excesses of the Supreme Court's decision in *Buckley v Valeo*, which equated campaign spending with speech. It will still allow people to spend their money, but it will make Terry Dolan of NCPAC responsible to speak—rather than let him hide behind little girls in yellow school buses. And it might encourage, because these ads will not be so plentiful, the media to do more coverage of campaigns, and cease abdicating their responsibility by virtue of the fact that they're selling time.

One question that constantly gets raised—isn't this abridging free speech, isn't this unconstitutional? I think it's constitutional. We are giving people the right to speak, to say whatever they want to in the marketplace. And we're forcing the opposition to say that these props are necessary and intrinsic to the exercise of free speech. In addition, Congress has the right to regulate elections constitutionally and to judge the qualifications of its own members. The courts have ruled that television is a different medium from all other mediums and in at least one decision has talked about the fact that television is to all other forms of communication as nuclear weapons are to conventional weapons. And beyond that, political advertising is not so different from commercial advertising, and commercial advertising has had a long history of being regulated.

As you evaluate such a proposal perhaps you might apply Ronald Reagan's standard. Would we be better off if it were enacted? Is the downside risk worse than its enactment? I think that the answer to the first question is yes, and the answer to the second is no.

Question: I want to make sure that when you are talking about patronage that you're also not endorsing things like awarding liquor store licenses, government contracts, high jobs, and other contracts and that sort of thing on this basis.

Charles Peters: You assume that with the liquor license or the bank charter that you need to regulate them. Stop and think of whether you really do. Open all these fields to free competition and you end the corruption because there will be no licenses or charters for corrupt officials to sell.

Race track dates in my state of West Virginia are one of the great sources of corruption. And what is really happening? The state is acting as a monopoly allotter, which is what's happening with all those licences and bank charters. If you take the state out of the business of allotting monopolies, then you don't have that corruption.

Obviously I'm against such corruption. But again, the whole point of my 50/50 system is clearly that there is something good about the civil service and clearly there is something good about the patronage system. You want to get both the goods, and try the best you can to protect yourself against the bad side of both.

What you have with the civil service is people who essentially aren't accountable, who aren't subject to being thrown out for bad performance. Their attention doesn't go primarily to delivering the mail because they aren't going to be fired if they don't deliver the mail. They aren't going to be fired if they just sit there chatting, and they know it. I want a system where there are enough people in there who care about performing and who know they can be thrown out. Do remember that with the old post office you got your mail twice a day in the thirties, and you got it delivered on time.

"What is the evidence that a system of democratic accountability would work better than the unaccountable civil service we have now? Those who were alive in the 1930s will remember that the post office delivered your packages intact and your letters on time, twice a day in fact. That postal system was political. If your mail didn't come on time you could complain to your congressman, and he would arrange for a new postmaster if he wanted to be reelected. The postal system became progressively less political in subsequent years and became completely non-political in 1968. What has happened to your mail? What happens when you complain now? You probably don't even bother, which is why the present bureaucracy is so discouraging to democracy—the citizen who speaks up knows he is wasting his time. He calls Federal Express instead."

—from "A Neoliberal's
Manifesto," *The Washington
Monthly,* May 1983

"The indifference to performance is not some abstract problem of public administration. It is central to the declining efficiency of both American industry and government. If you doubt me and happen to live in Washington, just remember the next time your bus breaks down and you're sweltering in the heat that Metrobus is forbidden to consider actual job performance in promoting its mechanics."

—from "A Neoliberal's
Manifesto," *The Washington
Monthly,* May 1983

BIBLIOGRAPHY

Articles in The Washington Monthly

Meyer, Richard, "Care for a Spin in My Chateau, Postmaster?" February, 1984

Riordan, Teresa, "Hatch 22," November, 1983

Longman, Phillip, "From Calhoun to Sister Boom Boom: The Dubious Legacy of Interest Group Politics," June, 1983

Crawford, Alan, "Government Unions and the Decline of the Work Ethic," January, 1983

Alter, Jonathan, "Ring Kissers and Empire Builders," March, 1982

Heard, Alex, "The Real Way to Save Our Cities," February, 1981

Palmer, Barbara, "The 10-to-3 Ethic," January, 1981

Reed, Leonard, "What's Wrong With Affirmative Action," January, 1981

Nelson, Michael, "Ten Ironies That Made Our Nation What It Is Today," November, 1980

Reed, Leonard, "The Joy of SES," July/August, 1980

Kaus, Robert M., "Zbig for Life," June, 1980

Easterbrook, Gregg, "The Art of Further Study," May, 1980

Reed, Leonard, "The Velvet Cage: The Life of a GS-15," September, 1979

Nocera, Joseph, "Inspectors General: The Fraud in Fighting Fraud," February, 1979

Kaus, Robert M., "How the Supreme Court Sabotaged Civil Service Reform," December, 1978

Reed, Leonard, "The Bureaucracy: The Cleverest Lobby of Them All," April, 1978

Nelson, Michael, "Bureaucracy: The Biggest Crisis of All," January, 1978

Reed, Leonard, "Firing a Federal Employee: The Impossible Dream," July/August, 1977

Chapman, Stephen J., "Inflated Pay," April, 1977

Reed, Leonard, "Inflated Job Descriptions," April, 1977

Boyd, Marjorie, "Inflated Grades," April, 1977

Fiorina, Morris P., "Big Government: A Congressman's Best Friend," March, 1977

Peters, Charles, "A Kind Word for the Spoils System," September, 1976

Dickson, Paul, "Delivering the Mail: We Did It Once and We Can Do It Again," July/August, 1976

Pincus, Ann, "How to Get a Government Job," June, 1976

Gourley, Jay, "The Bureaucrat's Country Club," May, 1976

Shapiro, Walter, "The Intractables," May, 1976

Peters, Charles, "The Firemen First Principle," March, 1976

Morris, Roger, "A Rare Resignation in Protest: Nat Davis and Angola," February, 1976

Anonymous, "A Day in the Life of a Government Executive," December, 1974

Redburn, Thomas, "Government Unions: The New Bullies on the Block," December, 1974

Shapiro, Walter, "Campaign Reform: Taking the Worry Out of Reelection," September, 1973

Paddock, William & Elizabeth, "So Hard to Remember, So Easy to Forget," February, 1973

Rothchild, John and Gonzales, Jack, "The Shriver Prescription: How the Government Can Find Out What It's Doing," November, 1972

Rappoport, Michael, "New Jersey: The People Close Their Eyes," February, 1972

Walton, Mary, "West Virginia: The Governor Tooketh," February, 1972

Lax, Eric, "The Culture of Bureaucracy: Nothing Fails Like Success," January, 1972

Rothchild, John, "Finding the Facts Bureaucrats Hide," January, 1972

Branch, Taylor, "Courage Without Esteem: Profiles in Whistle-Blowing," May, 1971

Haltersly, Roy, "The Anguish of Losing Office," February, 1971

Branch, Taylor, "We're All Working for Penn Central," November, 1970

Boyd, James, "Legislate? Who, Me?! What Happens to a Senator's Day," February, 1969

Books

Burns, James MacGregor, *The Power to Lead: The Crisis of the American Presidency*

Caro, Robert, *The Power Broker*

Hodgson, Geoffrey, *All Things to All Men*

Peters, Charles, *How Washington Really Works*

Shogan, Robert, *None of the Above*

Economic Growth

THE PANELISTS:

Michael Kinsley (moderator) is
The New Republic's TRB.
Mancur Olson, a professor of
political science at the
University of Maryland,
is author of
"The Logic of Collective
Action" and "The Rise
and Decline of Nations."
Donald Burr is president of People
Express airline.
Paul London, an economist, writes
frequently for
The New Republic
and other publications.
Peter Barnes, formerly the West
Coast editor of *The New
Republic,* is a self-described
"socialist entrepreneur."

Michael Kinsley (Moderator): Very briefly, let me
lay out the general themes of neoliberal writings on the
subject of the economy. As I read them, there are two
general themes. The first is a celebration of economic
growth itself. This has become so completely accepted that
it's not really novel any more, but ten years ago liberals

were saying nothing about economic growth. Someone in the audience put it very well this morning—"They make the money, and we liberals spend it." Liberals have got to think about how money is made. In that context, neoliberals tend to celebrate the small entrepreneur, the independent business person as opposed to, on the one hand the government, and on the other hand the large corporations.

The other vaguely neoliberal theme in economic writing goes by the term "industrial policy." This is the idea that the government must play a larger role, or a more specific role besides simply fiscal management and monetary management, in encouraging and discouraging certain industries. There's great controversy on that. Some neoliberals have championed such an industrial policy. Other neoliberals have written that this is a terrible idea.

Mancur Olson: The economic debate in this country, as in other countries, centers around the two familiar ideologies of right and left. The right-wing argument is that over-large government and over-generous aid to the poor impairs incentives to work and save and holds up economic growth. On the left we usually have the argument that we need more generous provisions for the poor and the use of industrial policy and similar devices to encourage the economy to perform better.

It occurred to me that it would be useful to test these ideas of right and left, debated so often and with so much passion, against the evidence of how well right-wing and left-wing governments have actually done in different countries and historical periods. Specifically, I decided to test how the size of the government and the extent of income redistribution to the poor correlated or failed to correlate with economic growth and prosperity. And I looked for the developed democratic countries that are comparable to our own in the years since WWII.

Looking at the evidence, I found that there was, quite clearly, no strong association in either direction. There was no pronounced tendency for either right-wing or left-wing governments to do much better than the other. And historically, one sees the same pattern with America. In the 19th century we had laissez-faire and great economic progress. So here's a case that accounts for the right. But between the World Wars we had pro-business governments and administrations such as those of Harding and Coolidge and Hoover—and bad results. The period after World War II, the period of the growth of the welfare state, was also, up until 1970, a period of unprecedentedly rapid growth. And that counts for the left. Adding it all together it surely does not constitute a clear pattern that should encourage either the right-winger or the left-winger to press ahead without further reflection and examination.

Why isn't there a strong pattern of evidence supporting either the right-wing or the left-wing point of view? The work I did for a recent book, "The Rise and Decline of Nations," I think helps a little bit at understanding the absence of these patterns. I begin the book talking about how it takes a long time to organize for collective action—to lobby for favors from the government, or form a combination or cartel that can influence prices or wages in the market. However, if the society has been stable for a long time, many such organizations will accumulate because, once they get started, they are very unlikely to disband, assuming there's no repression or violence that destroys them.

Special interest organizations do not try to make the country in which they find themselves better off, because each of these special interests is small in relationship to the country and its clients will get only a minute share of the benefits of making the country more prosperous. They try, rather, to get more for their own clients. And this, as I explain in this book, greatly reduces the efficiency and dynamism of the economy. An economy or society dense with special interest groups is a society that is like a china shop filled with wrestlers battling over its contents—and breaking much more than they carry away.

Any government, right or left, beholden to special interest organizations and supportive of cartels and collusions in the marketplace will work badly. The record shows both right-wing and left-wing governments alike, especially in countries like Great Britain and our own, correlated with, or governing over, economies that performed badly.

What intervention or interference in the market will do the most harm to an economy? Will it be intervention on behalf of the poor? Or will intervention that favors the already prosperous do the most harm? The moment we reflect on it, it becomes obvious that the poor, on the whole, are able to produce much less than the rich. So if the rich, or the most productive, are led not to produce that which the country needs most, but rather to seek loopholes or cartelization or other devices which do not add much to production, then we lose a very great deal. That in turn suggests that right-wing governments, often tied up with special interests representing the most prosperous and the most productive, will often, despite their useful rhetoric on behalf of free markets, intervene with those markets in the most harmful way.

Neoliberals should think of policy in terms of the reality that aiding the poor will have some cost besides the amount of dollars given to the poor; there will be some adverse effect on incentives. But the cost is largely going to be just a reduction in the amount of maid service and gardeners. But if a society offers the wrong incentives to the muscular people with blue collars doing important work in the factories of the country, that will indeed endanger the muscle of the economy. If a country aids its professions or distorts the incentives facing the professions, as we do in this country with the medicine and the law, it endangers the nerve system of the whole economy. And if, worst of all, with tariffs and bail-outs a country aids its great corporations, it lays down deposits of fat in the arteries leading to the heart.

As for industrial policy, I believe that a good principle — and I'd like to say even a neoliberal principle — is that the government ought to interfere where there is some kind of market failure. Most market failures arise because the good at issue has costs or benefits to people besides the people who buy and sell it; laissez-faire will not lead to clean air, for example. But the idea of an industrial policy of the more familiar sort, which would pick winners, seems a very bad idea. The one thing that governmental bureaucracy will be worst at is taking risks, and the way you get technological progress and industrial advance is, above all, by taking risks. Anyone who takes a risk and fails, of course, is in trouble. But the businessman who takes a risk and succeeds gets rich. The bureaucrat who takes a risk and succeeds is not going to get even any significant share of the benefits. So you ought to leave it to people who are in a situation where it's their own money that's lost if they make a mistake, and they are the gainers if they make a good pick.

Donald Burr: I think I'd do better if I just went over by the wall with a pad and took reservation requests. It's hard to talk about People Express or what's good about it with so many people unhappy about not being able to call it. Actually, we just have one little old lady with a telephone in a closet.

People Express is a phenomenon of some sort, and I would suggest that it's a message of hope. People Express has grown in a little over two years to be a business enterprise that generates around $400 million a year in revenues; within 12 months we estimate it will be a billion dollars of revenue. People is profitable in an industry not known for wonderful results—and lots of bankruptcies. During the period of time that People has done well, the other airlines have lost just under $5 billion. Several large airlines have gone under, and about 500 little ones have ceased to exist. And People Express has employed 3,000 people in an area of the country that has special interest groups all over, and I certainly share some of Professor Olson's views on that. They make it very difficult to do things.

We took the attitude, unlike, unfortunately, so many enterprises, that people basically are good and *want* to work, and that if you give them enough space and room they can find a way to be committed to it. That's the whole secret of People Express. It takes extraordinary amounts of commitment, not on the part of Don Burr, but on the part of hundreds of people who never even knew a Don Burr six months ago, or knew each other six months ago.

People Express has set out to create conditions for this commitment to happen. There are four pieces to this: the role of the individual, our precepts, our management practices, and our ownership.

A lot of people say People Express is somehow Japanese. But it's not Japanese at all. It's very, very Western in the sense that it epitomizes the role of the individual. In asking the individual to think about his or her commitment, we prescribe some general ideas about how we ought to behave. They're what we call precepts. The number one precept turns back on the individual again. It says that our number one job is to create a place where people can do well, defined in their terms. The number two precept is to try and be the best provider of airline transportation. Despite the fact that people cannot get through on the phones, People Express today, clearly on the numbers, is close to the best if it's not the best. It runs routinely with an 80 percent load factor, which is unheard of in the airline industry—and it does it month after month after month. Maximizing profits is not the number one precept of People Express; it's the number six precept and we never talk about it.

If you're talking about the commitment of an individual, you have to empower people to be able to work on their own, without supervision, without structures. So People Express is a very fluid place, with a very horizontal system where there are no supervisors. Nobody reports to anybody, so you've got 3,000 people walking around doing things. Yet it's got to be fairly organized.

Finally, we have an ownership system which is very important. Our people own an average of about $70,000 worth of People Express stock. Standing alone, I think that people who've had experience with this will be quick to tell you that owning something without a lot of other things going along with it is basically meaningless. But the fact that our people own a third of the company is a nice statistical fact; it's also a very important part of what we do and changes what people do to some degree. But if it weren't for all these other things involved, I don't think the ownership would make that big of a difference.

Paul London: Industrial policy is a great thing in war time, when you know what you want to do. But it seems to me when you don't know what to do, and that's clearly the case now, it creates more problems than it solves.

I'm a Democrat who thinks that economic growth, if we can figure out how to get it, is the most important thing for the country. It opens up a lot of possibilities. It seems to me that if we can find some way to grow, and that means growth without inflation, we can solve an awful lot of these problems that we're all concerned about and not make these openings for very conservative people like Ronald Reagan.

During periods of growth there's a great tendency in this country to slam on the brakes. You have a kind of chemotherapy—you kill all the cells in order to kill the ones that are running away. We did this in 1974, we did it again twice in the early 1980s. So we have to deal with the problem of inflation. But to do that, we have to ask ourselves not why oil prices go up—oil prices went up because OPEC made oil scarce—but why prices go up for things that aren't scarce? Why did wages go up in areas where workers weren't scarce, or where there were plenty of workers?

That's really the economic problem. And one of our big political-economic problems is that neither liberals nor conservatives really want to deal with that question: Why does a price or a wage go up when there is no scarcity? Conservatives instinctively don't want to deal with that problem because it suggests administered prices. Liberals don't want to deal with the problem because it puts them in the position of not only beating up on business—which a lot of liberals now don't like doing—but having to look at what unions are doing. So there's a strong tendency to fall back on, again, this kind of chemotherapy. We don't identify the culprits, the causes of inflation; we just sort of kill everything and hope that somehow, out of these ashes, the economy will grow again without inflation.

Let me give you an example of what I mean, based on an article I wrote for *The Washington Post* in August, 1983. The automobile companies announced at that time a $2\frac{1}{2}$ percent price increase. They also withdrew most of the rebates they were offering last year. So buyers are looking at sticker prices that, in effect, are 6 or 10 percent higher than they were a year ago.

The point I made in that article is that there wasn't a sound about this. For all the concern about inflation — we worry about budget deficits because somehow they will cause inflation, we worry about increases in the money supply because that will cause inflation — when somebody actually raises a price, nobody says anything. We seem to prefer to look at the shadow and not at the reality.

Almost at the time of this price increase, Chrysler's union workers got $2.00 an hour restored to them which they had given up a year and a half ago. People didn't say anything about this, either. It somehow seemed correct. Yet automobile workers now make 165 percent of the average wage and ten years ago they made only about 125 percent of the average wage. So autoworkers, with all of this unemployment and no scarcity — there are plenty of autoworkers around — get a $2.00 increase in wages.

The Japanese, I pointed out, followed an exactly opposite approach. During the 1970s the Japanese always went for greater market share. When it was very difficult for the Japanese to absorb changes in exchange rates that were making it costly to sell in the American market, Japanese automobile companies continued to sell in this market to increase their volume, even though it meant smaller and smaller profits.

That's what our automobile companies just passed up. They had a chance to lower prices to go for volume. They could have seized, in some sense, the moral high ground.

Likewise for the unions. In 1957 I came down to Washington to hear Walter Reuther of the United Auto Workers, who was speaking to the Kefauver Committee about "administered prices," a term that seems very apt but which we never use anymore. The automobile companies were just coming out of a serious recession. Walter Reuther said, I think what you ought to do is lower prices, go for volume, and we will take that into consideration when we make wage demands.

That ought to be the neoliberal platform. What the neoliberals ought to hold out to this country is growth with a moderation in wage increases. We ought to say that we want to promote growth, and that the way to do this is to make sure this growth goes to increased employment rather than increased wages.

The real issue in this country is not how much money goes to management and how much goes to labor, but how the labor part of the pie is divided. I think it's ominous that the labor part of the pie seems, certainly during the 1970s, to be divided more in favor of the upper part of the labor movement than the lower part, and that the upper part is becoming the constituency of the Democratic party. I worry about that a lot. I think we ought to have the labor constituency—and it ought to be all the workers.

Peter Barnes: My personal experience as an entrepreneur includes two start-ups in the last seven years of businesses that are 100 percent employee owned. The first of these, begun in 1977, was a solar energy design and contracting business in San Francisco that has since grown to employ about 25 people and have annual sales of approximately $2 million. The second business is a socially responsible money market fund called The Working Assets Fund.

When neoliberals talk or think about what they can do with their lives as well as their money—but specifically with their lives—to put into practice some of our values, I would like to add to the list of options being an entrepreneur. I have found this has not usually been on the list of options that liberals considered. But I tried it. I left journalism to go into the equally noble profession of being an entrepreneur, without a whole lot of training in business. My motivation, and I think this is true of many entrepreneurs, was not greed. It was to accomplish something, to put into practice many of the things that I believed in. Specifically, I wanted to deal with the energy crisis in a concrete way rather than just pointing to it as a problem.

Without trying to sound like a neoconservative, I think that the government was in many ways more of a pain in the ass than they were of any benefit. Still, there were several government programs that were valuable. The first was the CETA program, which no longer exists, for on-the-job training. We got a federally funded grant from a local agency that paid our small business half the cost of hiring and training a young solar installer. It was a very appropriate kind of program that enabled us to hire and train somebody we otherwise couldn't have. This woman ultimately became a vice president and the operations manager of our entire business, so it really was a great opportunity for her as well as us. Another government policy that was a benefit to our industry were the tax credits. Tax credits are a very powerful and effective tool when they are applied well. Obviously, they are subject to great abuses and there is this tendency, cited in one of the earlier panels, to give everybody tax credits for everything instead of targeting them creatively.

My vision of industrial policy is not of a group of wise people sitting in Washington picking winners. The chief goals of an industrial policy should be job creation, job preservation, and job satisfaction. The need for job crea-tion is obvious. (One thought has occurred to me—this is somewhat off the wall—why couldn't the government guar-antee to every young person who was a high school gradu-ate two years of a job after they graduated from high school, just the way that we, at least in California, guaran-tee to all high school graduates two years of community college?) Job preservation is also important because not every industry can be a dynamic-growth, sunrise industry. We need some mature industries and we have to have a policy for those as well. Job satisfaction, I think, is a critical part of industrial policy. It's directly related to productivity and the entrepreneurial energies we need to unleash, not just among a small elite of entrepreneurs, but among a very large segment of the working population.

The justification for our economic system has always been that if everybody pursued his or her own selfish interests, that somehow society as a whole would benefit, the total pie would grow. I think what neoliberals have correctly recognized is that while that may have been true in the past, it's no longer true. But we also have to recognize that unless we really deal with our economic system in a long-term, structural way, we're really not going to promote the values of sharing, responsibility, of community, of cooperation, of entrepreneurship, democracy, and equity that we have talked about. So for me a sensible industrial policy would go to the heart of the economic system, and would try to alter that system so the values we believe in are actually reinforced by the system rather than generally subverted. And a key aspect of such an industrial policy would be a series of steps to promote more worker ownership. I see that as one way to build structurally into our economic system some other values than just individual selfishness.

"The United States now has the highest percentage of obsolete plants, the lowest percentage of capital investment, and the lowest growth in productivity and savings of any major industrial society. Some reasons for our decline are obvious . . . But the current crisis has deeper roots. Simply put, the structure of our economy—its underlying organization, the incentives it offers—has discouraged long term growth in favor of short term paper profits. An ever-larger portion of our economic activity is focused on re-arranging industrial assets rather than on increasing their size. Instead of enlarging the economic pie, we are busy reassigning the slices.

"Look around you and you can see the rearrangers hard at work, prospering. They are the accountants who manipulate tax laws and depreciation rules to produce glowing—or at least presentable—annual reports. They are the financiers who think up new varieties of debentures or new mutual funds. They are the consultants who plot acquisition campaigns and the lobbyists skilled at obtaining government subsidies. They are corporate executives, trained in law and finance, who hire all of the above, and the lawyers whose briefcases bulge with the statutes, opinions, depositions, interrogatories, motions, and prospecti necessary to carry out their strategies."

—Robert Reich, "Pie-Slicers vs. Pie-Enlargers," *The Washington Monthly*, Sept. 1980.

BIBLIOGRAPHY

Articles in The Washington Monthly

Rowe, Jonathan, "Nobel Fever: Why the Engineers Left the Shop Floor," June, 1984

Rowe, Jonathan, "Weirton Steel: Buying Out the Bosses," January, 1984

Hammer, Charles, "Growth Without Inflation: Kennedy's Forgotten Prescription," December, 1983

Rowe, Jonathan, "The Cult of M1," November, 1983
Keisling, Phil, "Two Recessions Later: Why We Should Have Rationed
 Gas," July/August, 1983
Dorgan, Byron, "America's Real Farm Problem," April, 1983
Fallows, James, "The Gridlocked Society," March, 1983
Eisendrath, John, "How the IMF Makes the World Safe for Depression,"
 February, 1983
Alter, Jonathan, "Precarious Prosperity: The Siren Song of the Service
 Sector," December, 1982
Keisling, Phil, "Industrial America's Suicide Pact," December, 1982
Nocera, Joseph, "The Merger Mongers," December, 1982
Noah, Timothy, "Bring Back the WPA," September, 1982
Alter, Jonathan, "Defrocking the Fed," June, 1982
Easterbrook, Gregg, "How Big Labor Brings Home the Bacon," February,
 1981
Reich, Robert, "Pie-Slicers vs. Pie Enlargers," September, 1980
Kaus, Robert M., "Getting Tough on Trade," November, 1978
Lemann, Nicholas, "Independent Oil Men: Why They Take the Risks,"
 November, 1978
North, James, "The Economics of Extortion," November, 1978
Rosen, Corey, "How the Government Drove the Small Airlines Out of
 Business," June, 1977
Glassman, James K., "A Harvard Man Discovers Free Enterprise," October,
 1976
Peters, Charles, "Why Other Harvards Aren't Discovering It," October,
 1976
Winslow, John, "The Bankers' Attack on Free Enterprise," June, 1976
Redburn, Thomas, "Wall Street: The Entrepreneur's Worst Friend,"
 March, 1976
Ignatius, David, "Milton Friedman: The Ambiguous Achievement of a
 Positive Economist," December, 1975
Ignatius, David, "The Capital Crisis: Crying Wolf on Wall Street,"
 November, 1975
Peters, Charles and Allerhard, Glen, "The Case Against Energy Inde-
 pendence," September, 1975
Ignatius, David, "Shaking the Sheiks," January, 1975
Peters, Charles, "Putting Yourself on the Line," October, 1974
Shapiro, Walter, "How Not to Help Small Business," October, 1974
Winslow, John, "Big Is Bad For Us All," June, 1974
Samuelson, Robert, "Why Price Controls Stopped Working," May, 1974
Mintz, Morton, "Where They're Still Needed," May, 1974

Fallows, James, "How We Can Survive the Seventies," February, 1974
Lazarus, Simon, "Ralph Nader, the Last New Dealer," January, 1974
Rappoport, Michael and Van Lenten, Christine, "A Radical Proposal: Free Enterprise," May, 1973
Lessard, Suzannah, "Do Entrepreneurs Have More Fun?" December, 1972

Other Articles

Abernathy, William and Hayes, Robert, "Managing Our Way to Economic Decline," *Harvard Business Review,* July/August, 1980
Easterbrook, Gregg, "Voting for Unemployment," *The Atlantic,* May, 1983
Fallows, James, "American Industry: What Ails It, How to Save It," *The Atlantic,* September, 1980
Kaus, Robert M., "The Trouble With Unions," *Harper's,* May, 1983
Kaus, Robert M., "Can Creeping Socialism Cure Creaking Capitalism?" *Harper's,* February, 1983
Kinsley, Michael, "Tension and Release," *The New Republic,* February 7, 1981
Kinsley, Michael, "How to Save Capitalism from its Friends," *The New Republic,* March 15, 1980
London, Paul, "Does Anybody Still Believe in Competition?" *Washington Post Outlook,* August 21, 1983
Nocera, Joseph, "It's Time to Make a Deal," *Texas Monthly,* October, 1982

Books

Olson, Mancur, *The Rise and Decline of Nations*
           The Logic of Collective Action
Ouchi, William, *Theory Z*
Peters, Thomas and Waterman, Robert, *In Search of Excellence*
Reich, Robert, *The Next American Frontier*
Thurow, Lester, *Dangerous Currents*
           The Zero Sum Society

Critics' Panel

THE PANELISTS:
Morton Kondracke is executive
editor of
The New Republic.
Victor Navasky is the editor of
The Nation.
Irving Kristol is the editor of
The Public Interest.

Victor Navasky: Based on two days' exposure, it seems to me that I've heard almost as many definitions of neoliberalism as there are neoliberals. It's a little confusing to me. I'm going to give you some of the definitions — you've heard a couple already.

Morton Kondracke is reported to have said, "It's an attempt to combine the traditional democratic compassion for the downtrodden and outcast elements of society with different vehicles than categorical aid programs or quota systems or new federal bureaucracies."

Arthur Schlesinger, Jr., on the other hand, has called it "empty, a politically futile course for the Democratic party." The neoliberals, he has said, "have more or less accepted the Republican framework, they have joined in the clamor against big government, found great merit in the un-regulated marketplace, opposed structural change in the economy, and gone along with swollen military budgets in the nuclear arms race. Far from rejecting the Reagan framework, they would, at most, rejigger priorities here and there."

Senator Paul Tsongas has offered this definition: "Real-ism, some of it Republican in its origins, combined with a value system of the Democratic liberal tradition as the objective."

Economist Pat Choate says it's "really a study in prag-matism, of breaking past ideological boundaries to deter-mine how to restore long-term economic growth and to do it in a socially responsible and equitable manner."

Senator Eagleton said the idea had to do with automatic responses. Another member of the education panel this morning elevated it to the status of a party when she said that she didn't care which party was involved—Democrats, Republicans, or Neoliberals. Rick Hertzberg, editor of *The New Republic,* says that since the liberal side of the American sector—you all heard it today—desperately needs the creation of an ideology, that's why the neoliberal alter-native is an honorable task.

I am very grateful to have been here because I heard a lot of stimulating talk about cooperation and about community, particularly from Amitai Etzioni; about limits and echoes of the small is beautiful philosophy which I am attracted to. I heard refreshing formulations of ideas about the family, including the plight of feminists who also con-sider it important to raise children. And most of all I was moved by what I heard about the importance of voluntarism, except when it comes to the volunteer army, apparently.

I also heard disturbing talk about the need—this was from Mr. Yankelovich—to develop issues that don't carry the burden of liberal ideology from the past, as if the ideas of the Great Society had been tried and failed. In fact, it seems to me, they were scorned in the shadow of the Vietnam War and they never really had a chance. We don't know if they would fail if they were tried in the same atmosphere and with funding. I was in distress at the law panel as Mr. Kaus came out in the name of the "new realism" against all my favorite constitutional amendments. He would either amend or repeal, I'm not sure which, the Fifth Amendment, I think the Fourteenth Amendment, maybe the Fourth Amendment. And the way I heard the panel, some members would even like to make inroads on the First Amendment.

More disturbing than what I heard was what I didn't hear. I know a one-day conference can't cover everything and that there are a limited number of panels one can have. But the subjects chosen for coverage are the only evidence we have as to the priorities of this movement. Based on that standard, we may assume that Israel has either at long last come to terms with the Palestinians or that international affairs, in general, not to mention the problems in the Third World, don't really have a place in neoliberalism except insofar as they affect matters such as free trade on which our capitalist enterprises are so dependent. I heard nothing about the CIA's role in Nicaragua in particular or its involvement in covert action in general. The FBI had a holiday today. Earlier you were talking about *The Nation*, and it's true, if this had been a *Nation* conference, half the talk would have been about the FBI and the CIA, and that may be a limitation of ours. To find them absent in the agenda was culture shock to me.

If what we're talking about is, indeed, a movement and one dedicated to confronting reality, why does it have nothing to say about the fact that American corporations and their political and media allies dominate the political process, run the regulatory agencies, set Congressional agendas, determine the allocation of Pentagon contracts and outright subsidies in tax remission? Indeed, for too long this has been our unspoken industrial policy. And if it's a movement in touch with reality, whose reality is it? Is it really in touch with the reality of minorities and the poor?

I heard a lot about unions; every time someone said special interest groups, unions were at the top of the list. And they are a special interest. But I heard little in all the talk about economic democracy about the decline of unionism. I heard little about how it might be reversed and whether it ought to be reversed. And I heard little about how to ensure representation of workers within these unions that remain. Can it be that neoliberalism relies for its implementation on the erosion of labor strength? A serious question.

Above all, for me, there seemed to be an almost snobbish disinclination to talk about what it means to live with the knowledge and technology of mass destruction. I heard nothing about what it will mean for future generations brought up to assume and condone the possession of such weapons. Will they really be able to preserve the values and mutuality of compassion, of community and cooperation and of voluntary involvement in the affairs of their neighbors and their state that so many of the panels considered in other contexts?

Last night Charlie Peters said neoliberalism was a movement but he was unhappy with its name, so to end on a constructive note, I thought that I might make some suggestions. I was struck that very few people today mentioned the movement's most famous nickname—Atari Democrats. Can that be because of Atari's latest financial fortunes? If so, perhaps you will consider changing the name to Chrysler Democrats, or if it's not too old fashioned, Convertible Democrats.

I myself prefer "Charlie's Angels."

Irving Kristol: Charlie, stick with the name. The world gives you a name, take it and run with it. After all, I was called Irving. Don't be apologetic; it won't wash.

I think there really is such a thing as neoliberalism. I

think there really is such a thing as neoconservatism. I think there's such a thing as neoradicalism and neomarxism. And it's not only in America. In Europe as well you have neoconservatism; you have neoliberalism. The Social Democratic Alliance in Britain is a neoliberal movement. You will get it in Germany; you are getting it in France. We have an international phenomenon here. All of these neos came into existence for the same reason. They mean the original isms have run into a dead end. In the case of neoliberalism, the ism that has played itself out is liberalism, or to use a more accurate term, social democracy. What we call liberalism in this country really is an American version of social democracy, and in Europe and in the U.K. social democracy is undergoing exactly the same internal crisis as liberalism in this country, and the reaction is very much the same. So neoliberalism is up to something serious. I think it is a real movement; it's an intellectual movement.

Neoliberalism is a process of disengagement from social democratic liberalism, if I may use that phrase. It's also a disengagement from the upper middle class, Bohemian point of view which has been so popular in these last ten years and found many recruits within the liberal social democratic movement. It represents a disengagement from the limits to growth perspective that was so popular among liberals in the last 15 years.

You neoliberals are also in the process of disengaging yourself from certain traditional liberal views which are simply, in my view, anachronistic. Namely, it's the point of view that sees American society as dominated by large corporations, large unions, large government—a syndicalist society as described in John Kenneth Galbraith's books, which I used to assign to my class to read. I had to stop because I found they just lacked all credibility with the younger generation. I like neoliberalism's emphasis on small business, on entrepreneurship, and on the importance of economic growth. I think that is as distinct from economic distribution, though I'm not saying you have no emphasis on economic distribution. You do. But the emphasis on economic growth is a rediscovery of an important element of liberalism that got ignored over the past 15 years.

You do, of course, have your problems, just as we neoconservatives have our problems. You have an institutional problem which has been much remarked on at this meeting—namely, the trade unions. We have the corporate community. But in that sense we're much luckier than you are. The corporate community is much more manageable than the trade unions. The executives of large corporations are essentially apolitical. They want certain things from government, a limited number of things. Once they get them, they're not interested in politics. They have no political vision.

Trade unions are not like that. They are political institutions. Essentially, trade unions, not only in the United States but in all the countries of the world, have a syndicalist vision of the political future. The good society that all trade unionists envision is the society in which government controls the corporations and trade unions control the government. And that's what they're trying to get in Sweden, that's essentially what trade unionists want in the United States, that's what they want in France and England. It is, incidentally, a vision that goes back well over a hundred years, only the trade unionists have forgotten to articulate it. But they still have it. It's the only thing that explains why they do the things they do.

It's not going to be easy to cope with this syndicalist impulse within trade unions. Trade unions really want a corporate state. They like a corporate state. And if neoliberalism is opposed to a corporate state, as I assume it is, then neoliberalism is going to have to disengage itself from trade unions.

In foreign policy neoliberalism, so far as I can see, has not yet begun to do any thinking at all, really. Its instincts are stirring in the right direction, but the question of what America's role is in the world, whether or not we should be a great power with worldwide responsibilities, has not been addressed.

Neoliberals have a lot of perfectly sensible things to say about military reform, most of which I agree with. On the other hand, having reformed the military, what do you do with it? Presumably you have to use it somewhere. It's not clear to me where neoliberals want to use troops, under what circumstances, and for what purpose. But that's a very difficult problem because the truth is, liberalism itself never had a foreign policy, except for Woodrow Wilson, and we know what happened to that foreign policy.

One area where I think neoliberalism is very weak—though there are signs of movement there, too—is in culture and religion, especially religion. Neoliberalism, of course, like liberalism itself, regards religion as a private affair. That's the American conception of religion. But religion is needed by people, by all of us. A people without religion become ungovernable because a people without religion have no sense of the meaning of the world, have no sense of the reasonableness of what one can expect from the world. Though I don't see any hostility to religion in neoliberalism, I don't see much receptivity to it, either.

What is the future of neoliberalism? Well, neoconservatives have been helpful to you in many ways and will continue to be helpful to you in the future. Should the Democratic party win the next election, we will leave to you a very valuable legacy—namely, the budget deficit. Not all of it; we only claim half of it, that half generated by the tax cut and increased military spending. The other half is the recession and Congressional spending. But that half of the budget deficit would probably be our most valuable legacy to any future liberal administration since the Social Democratic liberals, the dominant trend in the party at the moment, really think in terms of Great Society programs. But they're not going to be able to apply that agenda; they're going to have to think of other things to do. In the course of thinking of other things to do, perhaps they'll turn to you for some ideas as to what might be done.

Should you win the next election, and I think you have a very good chance of doing that, you will, of course, be disillusioned. Neoliberals, like neoconservatives, are going to be disillusioned by the people they support. We've been disillusioned by Mr. Reagan. We got the original tax cut, and since then we've got nothing. As far as I'm concerned, there's recently been a weekend of critical importance in the history of the Reagan administration and journalists haven't even mentioned it. It's the first weekend that Ronald Reagan has gone golfing at a country club. He's become a country club Republican. I didn't even know he golfed. Neoconservatives have always felt, quite correctly, that within the Republican party their main enemy were the country club Republicans—the corporate executives who really don't want to have any political dynamism in our society and who really are 19th century liberals who want to be left alone so they can make money.

So you will be disillusioned. But you will survive, just as we're surviving.

Question: Two of the issues that neoliberals are trying to reconcile are community on the one hand and enterprise on the other hand. Traditionally, liberals and conservatives have made assumptions which were opposite. Conservatives have assumed

that enterprise takes care of community, that if everybody goes out and looks out for themselves the
invisible hand takes care of everything else. Liberals really haven't given a whole lot of thought to
the production and the creation of wealth, but rather
to the redistribution of the wealth that someone else
has taken the responsibility for creating.

I'd be interested in how you reconcile those two
things.

Kristol: The reconciliation is really quite easy.
Conservatives — and this is not just neoconservatives
— have always been able to reconcile entrepreneurship and economic dynamism with community precisely because of the assumption that religion would
take care of community. The most powerful single
source of community in the United States, from its
beginning, has been religion. All this talk about
community that leaves out religion is chatter. You
can have voluntary communities of small groups,
you can have communes if you want, but if you're
talking about community for large numbers of
working people, ordinary people, the center of
community has always been religion. Community
has generally centered around religion, and at the
same time we have had entrepreneurship and economic growth.

Navasky: I think there is a good example of religion
informing and improving enterprise — Reverend
Moon's operation is very profitable.

There's another way of thinking about community. Some young economists — David Gordon,
Samuel Bowles, and Thomas Weisskopf — have a book
out that talks about the importance of economic
democracy as the center of any attempt to deal with
the question of productivity. (*Beyond the Waste Land*,
Anchor/Doubleday) The only way of having a real
industrial policy that makes sense, they argue, is to

give workers not just an economic stake in it, but a real sense that they have control over their own destiny. And that has all kinds of implications for the possibility of community as well as the possibility of a very different kind of industrial policy than is generally thought of when people talk about it.

Kristol: You're looking for secular replacements for religion as the institution that really creates community. You want community in the work place. Well, maybe you can get it. But I've spent some of my time in the factory, and I don't believe it. I don't think workers go to the factory in order to seek out community. They work with a lot of people they don't like, they work with a lot of people whose values they don't share. You never discuss anything important in the work place. You never discuss religion, politics, or sex; that's the rule in any factory.

Question: Regardless of whether you call this a movement, a meeting, or whatever else, what is the most important thing in your opinion that "neo-liberalism" can bring to the American polity?

Navasky: I really think it's a word and not a movement, so I don't have an answer. And I think the thing to do is to recognize that and move on from there.

It does seem to me that all of the talk today about worker-owned enterprises, and to the extent that there was discussion of economic democracy, democracy in the work place, and a similar sense of participation in the school room—that's very important. And that is not going to happen from the top down by some order of some government agency. It is going to come from the bottom up, if it comes. It's the non-institutional communities that are the answer.

Kristol: I'd say both neoconservatives and neoliberals could perform a great service if, through their economic program, social program, and general mode of thinking they inspired the American people once again with faith in their institutions and hope for the future.

Morton Kondracke (Moderator): There are two different classes of things that we can do. One, since we do not have a Democratic candidate this time, so far as I can see, is to try to get as many ideas into the mix of Democratic issue discussion as we possibly can. That involves writing and trying to exert direct influence. The second thing to consider among ourselves is how to relate these ideas to any kind of a mass political base. We are, by and large, white middle class suburban people who have little connection with, and to some considerable degree I sense a certain amount of antagonism to, ordinary, factory-working Americans. If we have something that the mass of voters might want to involve themselves with, we have got to somehow discover what it is and how to put it into their terms.

Appendix:
A Neoliberal's Manifesto

Charles Peters
(*The Washington Monthly*, May, 1983)

If neoconservatives are liberals who took a critical look at liberalism and decided to become conservatives, we are liberals who took the same look and decided to retain our goals but to abandon some of our prejudices. We still believe in liberty and justice and a fair chance for all, in mercy for the afflicted and help for the down and out. But we no longer automatically favor unions and big government or oppose the military and big business. Indeed, in our search for solutions that work, we have come to distrust all automatic responses, liberal or conservative.

Perhaps nowhere have the liberal and conservative responses been more automatic than in the areas of welfare and crime. On welfare, the liberal tends to think all the poor (or practically all) are deserving, the conservative that they are bums and cheats who drive around in Cadillacs. The liberal bleeds for the criminal, blaming society for his crimes, and concocting exotic legal strategies to help him escape punishment. The conservative, on the other hand, automatically sides with police and prosecutor. Each group eagerly seizes on evidence that supports its position and studiously averts its eyes from any fact that might support the other side.

These automatic responses, by keeping us from facing any fact that might not fit them, mean that we aren't considering all the approaches that might help us solve our national problems. The inadequacies of the automatic response became dramatically obvious with the emergence of the problems that began to cripple the nation in the 1970s: declining productivity; the closed factories and potholed roads that betrayed decaying plants and infrastructure; inefficient and unaccountable public agencies that were eroding confidence in government; a military with too many weapons that didn't work and too few people from the upper classes in its ranks; and a politics of selfishness symbolized by an explosion of political action committees devoted to the interests of single groups.

Behind the liberals' inability to deal with these problems were four observable if unacknowledged principles.

The first was Don't Say Anything Bad About The Good Guy. The feeling here seemed to be that any criticism of institutions they liked—the public schools, the civil service, and the unions are good examples—was only likely to strengthen the hand of their enemies. A corollary was Don't Say Anything Good About The Bad Guys, meaning the police, the military, businessmen (unless small), and religious leaders (unless black or activist). What all this meant was a shortage of self-criticism among liberals and an unwillingness to acknowledge that there just might be some merit in the other side's position.

The second principle was Pull Up The Ladder. In both the public and private sector, unions were seeking and getting wage increases that had the effect of reducing or eliminating employment opportunities for people who were trying to get a foot on the first rung of the ladder. If, for example, more and more of the library's budget was used to pay higher and higher salaries for the librarians in the system, there would be little or no money to hire new librarians or even to replace those who left. So the result was not only declining employment but declining service. In the District of Columbia, libraries that were open 70 hours a week at the beginning of the decade were down to

40 hours by its the end. The city of Los Angeles has eliminated 1,995 jobs while radically reducing its street repaving and its library hours. At the same time it increased to 75 percent the proportion of its budget devoted to salaries and fringe benefits, including $93,688 to its fire chief and $98,908 to its police chief.

In the case of the auto and steel industries, the continuing wage increases meant that the industries became uncompetitive and went into decline. For a while all this meant was that the workers already on the ladder were doing better than ever. There just weren't any new jobs. Then as orders declined, layoffs followed and younger workers began dropping from the ladder. And, finally, as whole plants were closed, many of the fellows who had been pulling up the ladder found themselves out of work, too.

During this time too many liberals followed the Don't Say Anything Bad About The Good Guy principle, and refused to criticize their friends in the industrial unions and the civil service who were pulling up the ladder. Thus liberalism was becoming a movement of those who had arrived, who cared more about preserving and expanding their own gains than about helping those in need. Among this kind of liberal there is a powerful need to deny what they are doing, which means they become quite angry when it is exposed. When this magazine revealed that Washington's black upper class was pouring money into a fancy YMCA for its own use while neglecting the Y (now closed) that served poor blacks, there were howls of outrage. There is a similar reaction whenever we come close to suggesting that a poor black child might have a better chance of escaping the ghetto if we fired his incompetent middle-class teacher.

The third principle is The More The Merrier. The assumption here—and it is often correct—is that the more beneficiaries there are of a program, the more likely it is to survive. Take Social Security. The original purpose was to protect the elderly from need. But, in order to secure and maintain the widest possible support, benefits were paid to rich and poor alike. The catch, of course, is that a lot of money is wasted on people who don't need it.

Similarly, the original justification for the tax breaks for capital gains and mortgage interest was that they would stimulate investment in new plants and new housing, thereby creating new jobs. But the breaks were also given to trading in stocks that represented only existing plants and to trading in existing housing. This cost the treasury a bundle and the only new jobs it created were for stock and real estate brokers.

The fourth principle is Politics Is Bad And Politicians Are Even Worse. Liberalism entered the seventies having just depoliticized the last refuge of patronage, the post office. The catch was that in destroying patronage—the last nail in the coffin was a mid-seventies Supreme Court decision that actually held it was unconstitutional to fire a political appointee for political reasons—no one noticed that democracy was the first casualty. If democracy means we are governed by people we elect and people they appoint, then it is a not insignificant fact that the people we elect can now choose less than one percent of those who serve under them. Without the lifeblood of patronage, the political parties have withered and been replaced by a politics of special interest. And since liberals assumed that patronage was always bad, they could see no answer to the problem.

Opposed to these four principles of the old liberalism are the primary concerns of neoliberalism: community, democracy, and prosperity.

Economic growth is most important now. It is essential to almost everything else we want to achieve. Our hero is the risk-taking entrepreneur who creates new jobs and better products. "Americans," says Bill Bradley, "have to begin to treat risk more as an opportunity and not as a threat."

We want to encourage the entrepreneur not with Reaganite policies that simply make the rich richer, but with laws specifically and precisely designed to help attract investors and customers. For example, Gary Hart is proposing a "new capacity" stock, a class of stock issued "for the explicit purpose of investment in new plants and equipment." The stock would be exempt from capital gains tax on its first resale. This would give investors the incentive they now lack to target their investment on new plants and equipment instead of simply trading old issues, which is what most of the activity on Wall Street is about today.

We also favor freeing the entrepreneur from economic regulation that discourages desirable competition. But on the matters of health and safety, we know there must be vigorous regulation, because the same capitalism that can give us economic vitality can also sell us Pintos, maim employees, and pollute our skies and streams.

Our support for workers on health and safety issues does not mean support for unions that demand wage increases without regard to productivity increases. That such wage increases have been a substantial factor in this country's economic decline is beyond reasonable doubt. But—and this is a thought much more likely to occur to neoliberals like Lester Thurow than to neoconservatives—so have ridiculously high salaries for managements that show the same disregard for performance. The recently resigned president of International Harvester was being paid $1.4 million a year as he led his company to the brink of disaster.

We also oppose management compensation that encourages a focus on short-term profit instead of long-term growth. And we favor giving the worker a share in the ownership of his company.

In this connection, a perfect example of the neoliberal approach was provided by Paul Tsongas during the Senate debate over the Chrysler bailout. The United Auto Workers sought guaranteed wage increases for its members. Tsongas objected. Why should a company on the verge of bankruptcy pay wage increases? On the other hand, Tsongas realized that workers would feel exploited if their efforts produced profit for the company and it all went to the shareholders. The Tsongas solution was to give the workers stock instead of money. If their efforts helped save the company, they would not be suckers, they would share in the success.

Another way we depart from the traditional liberal's support for organized labor is in our criticism of white-collar unions for their resistance to performance standards in the evaluation of government employees. We aren't against government, period, as—with the exception of the national security apparatus—many conservatives appear to be. But we are against a fat, sloppy, and smug bureaucracy. We want a government that can fire people who can't or won't do the job. And that includes teachers. Far too many public school teachers are simply incompetent.

Our concern about the public school system illustrates a central element of neoliberalism: It is at once pragmatic and idealistic.

Our practical concern is that public schools have to be made better, much better, if we are to compete economically with other technologically advanced countries, if we are to have more Route 128s and Silicon Valleys. Our idealistic concern is that we have to make these schools better if the American dream is to be realized. Right now there is not a fair chance for all because too many children are receiving a bad education. The urban public schools have in fact become the principal instrument of class oppression in America, keeping the lower orders in their place while the upper class sends its children to private schools.

Another way the practical and the idealistic merge in neoliberal thinking is in our attitude toward income maintenance programs like Social Security, welfare, veterans' pensions, and unemployment compensation. We want to eliminate duplication and apply a means test to these programs. They would all become one insurance program against need.

As a practical matter, the country can't afford to spend money on people who don't need it — my aunt who uses her Social Security check to go to Europe or your brother-in-law who uses his unemployment compensation to finance a trip to Florida. And as liberal idealists, we don't think the well-off should be getting money from these programs anyway — every cent we can afford should go to helping those really in need.

The pragmatic idealism of neoliberals is perhaps the clearest in our reasons for supporting a military draft.

A draft would be a less expensive way to meet our need for military manpower because we would no longer have to use high salaries to attract enlistees. It would also be the fairest way, because all classes would share equally in the burdens and risks of military service.

Those who are drafted and opposed as a matter of conscience to military service should have the option of entering a domestic or overseas peace corps. But if that option is taken, the term of service should be three years instead of two; this should help guarantee that the decision is in fact one of conscience. In the long run we hope a draft will not be needed. We want to see a rebirth of the spirit of service that motivates people to volunteer to give, without regard to financial reward, a few years of their lives to public service, including military service. But for now we realize that the fear of being a sucker, if not just plain selfishness, will keep the upper classes from volunteering.

There is another reason for our support of a draft at the present time. We want to bring people together. When I was growing up, social classes were mixed by both the public schools and the draft. Today the sons of the rich avoid the public schools and scorn the military service. This is part of a trend toward separatism — not only by race but by class and interest group — that has divided the nation and produced the politics of selfishness that has governed this country for more than a decade.

The rise in the power of the interest-group lobbies has been accompanied by an increase in single-issue politics, with misleading oversimplifications of the other side's position — as on abortion, for example — and a tendency on both sides to judge a politician solely by his stand on this one matter.

I think the only possible salvation for this republic is a citizenry that is determined to inform itself on a broad range of important issues — and that will vote for an elected official on the basis of his or her stand on *all* the issues. We now have a Congress that is petrified of offending any single, passionate group — be they private boat owners or banks — and that won't change until the members know we're not going to throw them out of office on any basis other than overall performance.

The only way to destroy the escalating power of the lobbies is to destroy single-issue politics. Today everyone is imitating the National Rifle Association. That's the way to have a successful lobby. It's also the way to ruin America.

We have made dividing ourselves against ourselves into a virtue. While it is certainly necessary at times, the adversary approach to problems has come to dominate our national life, at a disastrous cost to all of us.

In industry, our adversarial system has been a major

factor in making our corporations less efficient than their foreign competition. In Japan auto workers think about how they can improve their products; in America, they think about filing grievances. In theory the adversarial relationship between management and labor is supposed to act as a guarantee against antisocial behavior by either. In the seventies, however, it resulted in both sides taking what they wanted. And in such basic industries as steel and automobiles, this meant that we priced ourselves right out of an ability to compete with foreign producers.

The adversary relationship between Congress and the White House all too often paralyzes government. It has led to a situation where Congress cannot trust the information provided by the executive branch. As a result Congress has set up its own bureaucracy, including a budget office, to develop the same information that is supposed to be provided by federal agencies.

Finally, the adversary system of justice helps to create a society where differences are magnified, breeding suspicion and mistrust, instead of calmly reconciled. That's why we favor a no-fault approach to two of the major court-cloggers—divorce and auto accidents—and the use of mediation in most other cases. Mediators would not have to be lawyers. They could be elected by their neighbors or selected by the parties to the dispute.

Our reason for opposing a law degree as a requirement for mediators brings us to another fundamental tenet of neoliberalism. We have only the most modest regard for degrees or other paper credentials. People should be judged on their demonstrated ability to perform, not on their possession of a piece of parchment. The ultimate silliness of credentialism was revealed last year when a former major leaguer was for a time denied the right to coach high school baseball because he lacked a teaching certificate. The major leaguer was finally hired, but only, I suspect, because sports and the performing arts are the last areas of American life in which demonstrated ability is the only test for hiring, firing, and promotion.

If he had been looking for a job as an English teacher, a demonstration of superior knowledge of and ability to impart that subject to the young would probably have gotten him nowhere without an education degree. The irrelevance of the education degree to actual teaching ability is suggested by the fact that the degree is not required by the best private schools. What they care about is that the teacher can teach. Neoliberals share this concern with actual performance because they want to encourage productivity and discourage the bureaucratization that credentialism fosters and that has become one of the most severe problems in our government and in our large corporations.

The search for credentials is also undermining our economic prosperity. During the past academic year, 127,530 men and women were enrolled in law schools. These are among our ablest young people. If they had chosen productive work, they would have been on the cutting edge of the economic recovery we so desperately need. Instead, they spent the year sitting in some library, trying to focus their eyeballs on *Corpus Juris*. We have 15 times more lawyers per capita than Japan. Japan, with a population half our own, produces twice as many engineers a year.

"Anthropologists of the next century," Michael Kinsley has observed, "will look back in amazement at an arrangement whereby the most ambitious and brightest members of each generation were siphoned off the productive work force, trained to think like a lawyer, and put to work chasing one another around in circles."

Seniority is another enemy of the performance standard. Take the way the government has been carrying out its RIFs (reductions in force). People are being fired, not for lack of ability but for lack of seniority. Someone who has been around a long time can "bump" a younger employee even when the junior official is much more talented and dedicated.

This indifference to performance is not some abstract problem of public administration. It is central to the declining efficiency of both American industry and government. It even affects everyday life. If you doubt me and happen to live in Washington, just remember the next time your bus breaks down and you're sweltering in the heat that Metrobus is forbidden to consider actual job performance in promoting its mechanics.

The Reagan administration, to its great credit, is trying to do something about this, trying in the words of one official "to make job performance the center of the federal personnel system." Neoliberals will support this effort. We are generally against Reagan's policies but not automatically so. Lincoln explained our reasoning in his speech in Peoria:

"Some men, mostly Whigs, who condemn the repeal of the Missouri Compromise, nevertheless hesitate to go for its restoration, lest they be thrown in company with the abolitionist. Will they allow me as an old Whig to tell them good-humoredly, that I think this is very silly? Stand with anybody that stands RIGHT. Stand with him while he is right and PART with him when he goes wrong. To desert such ground, because of any company, is to be less than a Whig—less than a man—less than an American."

A REVIVAL OF POLITICS

Snobbery, like the credentialism to which it is related, is another neoliberal target. The snobbery that is most damaging to liberalism is the liberal intellectuals' contempt for religious, patriotic, and family values. Instead of scorning people who value family, country, and religion, neoliberals believe in reaching out to them to make clear that our programs are rooted in the same values.

Take school prayer. While I easily can see how the custom of my youth, requiring children to recite the Lord's Prayer at the beginning of school, was offensive to nonbelievers, I also can see no reason to oppose a few minutes of silent meditation. During such a period those who want to pray can pray, and those who don't want to pray can think about baseball (which I often managed to do while reciting the Lord's Prayer), or anything else sectarian or nonsectarian they want to think about. If the teacher tries to make them pray, fire him. But there is absolutely nothing wrong—indeed there is great good—in asking young people to think quietly for a few moments about the meaning of it all. Yet many liberals see the prayer issue as one of the seminal battles of the enlightenment against the "hicks."

It is this contempt for the "hicks" that is the least appealing trait of the liberal intellectuals. Many of them, we have seen, don't really believe in democracy. Neoliberals do—we think a lot of those hicks are Huck Finns, with the common sense and good will to make the right choices if they are well informed.

Informing them properly means giving them a better education in politics and government, not just in the schools, but through the press. This in turn requires better teachers and reporters than we have now, teachers and reporters who know the history of the American political system and the lessons of its successes and failures—subjects largely ignored in our teachers colleges and journalism schools. Even in our most elite universities, few courses are organized in a way that permits the student to ponder, for example, the contrast between the Bay of Pigs and the Cuban missile crisis.

Since experience is the best teacher of all, if we truly are going to reform the American system of government, we need to give more Americans experience in government. We need more politics, not less—more good people running for office. Unfortunately, the worst form of snobbery in America today is the smug assumption that politics and politicians are inherently bad.

If you think for a moment about the kind of choices we've had in recent elections, you'll realize why we must have a lot more good people pursuing political careers. This in turn means offering enough opportunities to attract people to a life in politics. Today a person who starts out in politics has a tiny field of opportunity in the federal government—congressman, senator, president, and just 2,000 appointive positions.

What if we opened hundreds of thousands of federal jobs to political appointees, replacing through normal attrition roughly half the federal government's 2.8 million civilian employees? Give the new people two-and-a-half year appointments, with a limit of five years on the time they would be permitted to remain in government.

This would bring people with real-world experience into government, attract more risk-takers not obsessed with job security and provide a legitimate reward for political participation. If we don't want a system that runs on money, then we have to offer something else. What is better to offer to the people who push the doorbells and hand out the leaflets than the opportunity to participate in putting into effect the programs they have campaigned for? Their reward would be legitimate because the unqualified would not profit from it. Your sister Suzie who can't type 50 words a minute would not be allowed to get that government typing job no matter how hard she worked in your campaign.

Because the jobs would be limited to a few years, we also would be constantly sending back into the ranks of the voting public people who have learned firsthand why Washington doesn't work and who have nothing to lose from speaking out about the reforms that are needed.

My God, you say, what if Reagan could begin making these appointments now? The answer is that you could vote him out next year and elect a president who would have both the right program and the power to put it into effect. And you would realize that accountable government won't work unless you are an accountable voter, so you would never again cast your vote carelessly or simply fail to go to the polls altogether.

There is no question, however, that restoring power to our elected officials does mean we have to watch them more carefully. That's why we need intelligent and diligent reporting, and that's why I would keep roughly half of government positions in the civil service. That leaves someone there to blow the whistle when the politicians go wrong, as sometimes they are bound to do. Civil servants would also provide continuity and institutional memory that would otherwise be lacking. But surely 50 percent can do that and still leave the other jobs to provide incentives for people to participate in politics and a dramatic increase in the number of people who understand the government.

If this approach had been in effect for even a decade, we would have a nation far better equipped to appraise the budget cuts that are said to be needed, who would have the sophistication to know exactly where to find them. We would have people in government who, because they'd spent most of their lives on the outside, would have genuine empathy for the problems of those on the outside. The lack of such empathy has been the most glaring deficiency of the bureaucracy in Washington.

What is the evidence that a system of democratic accountability would work better than the unaccountable civil service we have now? Those who were alive in the 1930s will remember that the post office delivered your packages intact and your letters on time, twice a day in fact. That postal system was political. If your mail didn't come on time you could complain to your congressman, and he would arrange for a new postmaster if he wanted to be reelected. The postal system became progressively less political in subsequent years and became completely nonpolitical in 1968. What has happened to your mail? What happens when you complain now? You probably don't even bother, which is why the present bureaucracy is so discouraging to democracy—the citizen who speaks up knows he is wasting his time. He calls Federal Express instead.

One problem of the new liberal is the way he is misunderstood by the old liberals. I am sure that most of them have read what I have written here as advocating a return to the days of the Vietnam draft, robber barons, Tammany patronage, and coerced prayer. I have, of course, advocated none of those things. In each case I have said something different, and it is important that the old liberals attend to the difference.

At the same time, the new liberal must be willing to risk misunderstanding. Risk is indeed the essence of the movement—the risk of the person who has the different idea in industry or in government. That is why we place such a high value on the entrepreneur. The economic, social, and political revitalization we seek is going to come only through a dramatic increase in the number of people willing to put themselves on the line, to take a chance at losing all, at looking ridiculous.

Risk-taking is important not only in career terms but in the way one looks at the world and the possibilities it presents. If you see only a narrow range of choices, if you are a prisoner of conventional, respectable thinking, you are unlikely to find new ways out of our problems. Neoliberals look at the possibilities with a wide-angle lens. For example, some of us, who are on the whole internationalists and free-traders, are willing to consider such bizarre ideas as getting out of NATO, forgetting about the Persian Gulf, and embargoing Japanese cars.

One problem we're trying to address with such suggestions is that American industry's ability to compete has been seriously impaired by the amount of money we have spent in the common defense compared to our competition and that we must find some dramatic way to redress the balance.

But if neoliberals were to support an embargo on Japanese cars, it would be only for the time necessary to get the auto industry back on its feet and it would be conditioned on the willingness of management to cut prices to competitive levels and of labor to accept the wage reductions necessary to make the price cuts possible. Neither would agree to such steps now, but the fact that they are more open to such ideas than they were just a few years ago is one of the signs I see of a national movement toward neoliberalism.

You can find these signs in the fields of national defense, income security, and criminal justice as well in changing attitudes toward labor and management.

In the case of labor, the most heartening evidence has to be Weirton Steel, where the workers accepted a 32 percent wage cut to keep their company alive. They will not be suckers because they will own the plant and share in the future profits their sacrifice makes possible. It's better for a worker to keep a job by accepting $12 an hour than to lose it by insisting on $19. We specifically reject the Atari Democrat label, because we think such wage adjustments could mean our economic future lies just as much in revitalized basic industries as in high technology. The People Express Airlines model provides another hopeful sign. All the employees own stock, they are not bound by union restrictions on what they can and can't do and can pitch in wherever needed, and the result is the company is prospering in an industry that otherwise isn't.

People Express is also an example of neoliberal ideas in management. Its founder, Donald Burr, risked his entire savings on the enterprise. Hierarchy and bureaucracy are not favored; entrepreneurial, creative behavior and democratic organization are. And Burr extols the crucial importance of "making everything the common concern of all."

Other signs of neoliberal infiltration into management thinking are the growing contempt for merger-mania and its practitioners like William Agee; the rise to the top of the best-seller list of *In Search of Excellence,* a book excerpted here in December that describes successful companies as those that encourage innovation, risk-taking, and experimentation rather than constant study, traditional chains of command, and playing it safe; the widespread acceptance of the Robert Hayes-William Abernathy indictment of the hired-gun MBA and his focus on short-term results that bring luster to his resume and disaster to his company; and the increasing attention given to Robert Reich's emphasis on expanding the economic pie as against merely rearranging its slices. When Reich was published here, he was reaching 35,000 subscribers. But now his work appears in *The Atlantic,* where it reaches ten times that audience.

Other positions taken in the past by *The Washington Monthly* are now becoming respectable wisdom. One is that liberals should not content themselves with merrily opposing increases in defense spending but should find out on what weapons money is being wasted and on what weapons more should be spent. In other words, identify both the turkeys and today's equivalents of Britain's Spit-fire in World War II, the weapons that we need to survive. Another is that the insanity defense is itself insane and that violent criminals, sane or insane, should be locked up on the basis of the danger they pose to society.

When we first planted our flags on these positions and looked around for the army we hoped was following, the field behind us was, if not totally empty, certainly not at all crowded. Now almost every day's paper brings a new evaluation of a weapons system. And both the American Psychiatric Association and the American Bar Association are attacking the insanity defense.

On the income-security issue, the neoliberal approach has won small but significant victories as taxes were enacted in 1979 and this year on unemployment compensation and Social Security income above certain levels. These are steps toward the means test we advocate for all income maintenance programs. Our opposition comes from two sources. One is the Brookings Institution-type liberal who sees only incremental reform as realistic and therefore refuses to take radical solutions seriously. Then there are the old liberals who see a means test as hurting the feelings of the recipient. This could be called the Don't Embarrass Little Orphan Annie principle. The recipient is always seen as some pathetic child who would be humiliated to have to hold up his hand and say, "Teacher, my Mother and Daddy can't afford to pay for my lunch so can I please have one of those free school lunches for poor people?"

Neoliberals don't want children to endure such an experience either, and we oppose programs that require them to do so. But, by the time someone is an adult, shouldn't he be able to face reality, and say, I need help because I'm poor? Is not facing reality at the very heart of adult responsibility?

So we've traveled some of the way along the path. And

that's good. But, frankly, I doubt if we'll make it the rest of the way without a rebirth of patriotism, a rebirth of devotion to the interests of the national community, of the conviction that we're all in this together and that therefore fair play and justice for everyone is the vital concern for us all. Robert McElvaine captured the model that should guide us in *Down and Out: Letters From the Forgotten Man in the Great Depression:*

"In letters that 'ordinary' Americans wrote during the 1930s, the overwhelming emphasis was upon themes of fairness and the necessity of justice. 'We are Poor People,' a group of Maryland WPA workers wrote to President Franklin D. Roosevelt in 1936, 'but we are human. We wish to be treated that way.' They went on to say, 'We feel you'll give us justice.' Similar sentiments were echoed in thousands of Depression-era letters. 'I knows and think that you feels our care and means right,' an anonymous correspondent wrote to F.D.R. in 1935, 'and you will do what is right if you knows the suffering of the people.' . . .

"The evidence that the major—although certainly not the exclusive—thrust of the current generation is toward extreme egotistical individualism is abundant. But the shift in values is not absolute. In all eras—and in most individuals—selfishness and compassion coexist. It is the mix of the two that varies. There is a tendency for the former to be more prevalent among the affluent, particularly if they are still on the rise or their positions are threatened . . .

"Seen in this light, the basic difference between the dominant values of the 1930s and the 1980s is that much of the middle class in the earlier period identified with the poor, whereas the bulk of Middle America now aspires to become like the rich. The Joads of *The Grapes of Wrath* sought survival and a decent life; the Joneses seek not merely to keep up with each other, but to emulate the

Rockefellers to whatever extent possible."

During World War II, FDR proposed a $25,000 limit on all salaries. He saw the danger that people would lose the idealism of the struggle against depression and tyranny and become preoccupied with personal gain, that they would begin to forget about the national interest in pursuit of their own.

FDR may have been wrong in thinking people didn't have the right to get rich, but he was sublimely right in understanding that they shouldn't forget their nation and their fellow man in the process.

The title of *You Can't Take It With You,* the recently revived thirties comedy by Moss Hart and George S. Kaufman suggests another value underlying the $25,000 limit. The play is about the Sycamores and their household, a group of people who have risked making fools of themselves in the eyes of the respectable world, symbolized by the rich Kirbys, in order, in the director's words, "to fulfill their dreams as opposed to being in the rat race of keeping up with the Joneses and putting money as a symbol for success above everything else."

The Sycamores are, to say the least, a remarkably diverse group, but they all show great tolerance and good humor in dealing with one another. They don't pull up their ladder, they extend it to the world—finally even to the Kirbys, who need it spiritually, if not financially.

In many ways life was much tougher in the thirties than it is today, but there was, incredibly enough, a lot more sunshine in the soul and a lot more laughter in the land. That spirit is the heart of neoliberalism. Without it, we will never overcome the politics of self-righteous, self-pitying interest groups. With it, we can begin to listen to one another, rebuild community, and take the risks that can produce the just and prosperous democratic society we all want.